CAMPAIGN 308

ST LÔ 1944

The Battle of the Hedgerows

STEVEN J. ZALOGA   ILLUSTRATED BY JOHNNY SHUMATE

Series editor Marcus Cowper

First published in Great Britain in 2017 by Osprey Publishing,
PO Box 883, Oxford, OX1 9PL, UK
1385 Broadway, 5th Floor, New York, NY 10018, USA
E-mail: info@ospreypublishing.com

Osprey Publishing, part of Bloomsbury Publishing Plc

OSPREY is a trademark of Osprey Publishing, a division of Bloomsbury
Publishing Plc.

A CIP catalog record for this book is available from the British Library.

Print ISBN: 9781472816931
PDF e-book ISBN: 9781472816948
ePub e-book ISBN: 9781472816955
XML ISBN: 9781472822802

Index by Fionbar Lyons
Typeset in Myriad Pro and Sabon
Maps by Bounford.com
3D BEVs by The Black Spot
Originated by PDQ Media, Bungay, UK
Printed in China through World Print Ltd.

17 18 19 20 21 10 9 8 7 6 5 4 3 2 1

AUTHOR'S NOTE

For brevity, the traditional conventions have been used when referring to
units. In the case of US units, 2/39th Infantry refers to the 2nd Battalion,
39th Infantry Regiment. The US Army traditionally uses Arabic numerals for
divisions and smaller independent formations (9th Division, 743rd Tank
Battalion), Roman numerals for corps (VII Corps), spelled-out numbers for
field armies (First US Army). In the case of German units, 2./GR 919 refers to
the 2nd Company, Grenadier-Regiment 919; II./GR 919 indicates the 2nd
Battalion of Grenadier-Regiment 919. German corps were designated with
Roman numerals such as LXXXIV Armee Korps, but the alternate version 84
AK is used here for clarity. Field armies were designated in the fashion 7.
Armee, but sometimes abbreviated in the fashion AOK 7; the former style is
used here.

Unless otherwise noted, all photographs in this book are from official US
sources including the National Archives and Records Administration, US
Army Military History Institute, Library of Congress, and US Army Patton
Museum. The author would like to thank Kevin Hymel for his kind help on
this book.

Osprey Publishing supports the Woodland Trust, the UK's leading woodland
conservation charity. Between 2014 and 2018 our donations are being
spent on their Centenary Woods project in the UK.

To find out more about our authors and books visit
www.ospreypublishing.com. Here you will find extracts, author
interviews, details of forthcoming events and the option to sign up for
our newsletter.

GLOSSARY

AOK	*Armeeoberkommando*: army high command, common abbreviation for a German field army
AR	Artillerie-Regiment
FJR	*Fallschirmjäger-Regiment*: paratrooper regiment
GFM	*Generalfeldmarschall*: field marshal
GMC	Gun Motor Carriage, often a tank destroyer
GR	*Grenadier-Regiment*
MHI	Military History Institute, Army Historical Education Center, Carlisle Barracks, PA
NARA	National Archives and Records Administration, College Park, MD
OB West	Oberbefehlshaber West: High Command West (Kluge's HQ)
PaK	*Panzerabwehr Kanone*: anti-tank gun
SHAEF	Supreme Headquarters, Allied Expeditionary Force (Eisenhower's HQ)
tonne	Metric ton (2,205 pounds)

Key to military symbols

××××× Army Group	×××× Army	××× Corps
×× Division	× Brigade	III Regiment
II Battalion	I Company/Battery	Platoon
Section	Squad	Infantry
Artillery	Cavalry	Airborne
Unit HQ	Air defense	Air Force
Air mobile	Air transportable	Amphibious
Antitank	Armor	Air aviation
Bridging	Engineer	Headquarters
Maintenance	Medical	Missile
Mountain	Navy	Nuclear, biological, chemical
Ordnance	Parachute	Reconnaissance
Signal	Supply	Transport movement
Rocket artillery	Air defense artillery	

Key to unit identification

Unit identifier / Parent unit / Commander

(+) with added elements
(-) less elements

CONTENTS

The Strategic Situation, July 3, 1944

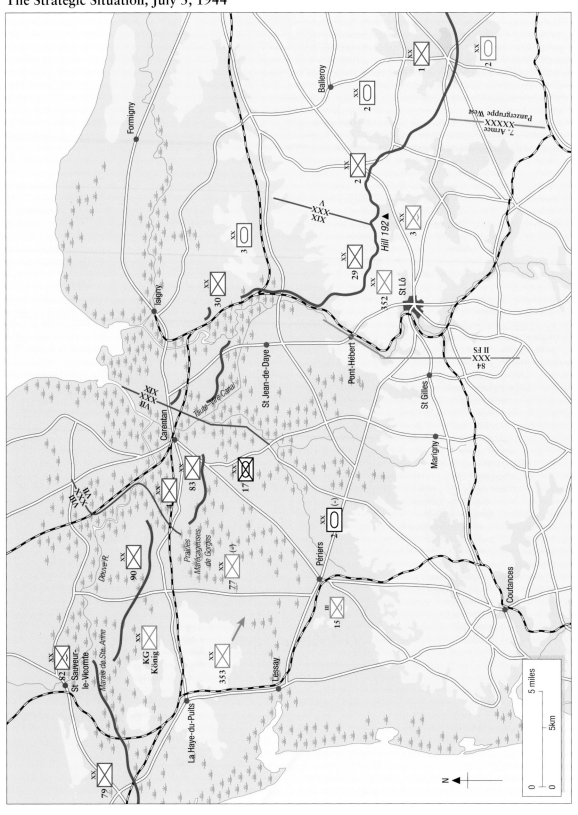

INTRODUCTION

General Dietrich von Choltitz, described the Battle of the Hedgerows as "a monstrous blood-mill, the likes of which I have not seen in my eleven years of battle." This three-week campaign in July 1944 was a series of relentless small-scale skirmishes in the countryside north east of St Lô. For the US Army, the objective was to push out of the constricted coastal low-lands south of Omaha Beach to reach terrain better suited for a mechanized break-out. Aside from the immediate terrain objectives, the campaign was also intended to decimate the Wehrmacht in Lower Normandy to ensure the success of the eventual break-out. From the German perspective, the mission was to bottle up the US Army in the hedgerow country around the Vire River since the terrain was far more suitable for defense than the countryside further south. By the third week of July, the First US Army had reached far enough south to stage the break-through, and the German 7. Armee had suffered such exceptional losses that it was on the verge of being routed. On July 25, 1944, the First US Army initiated Operation *Cobra*, starting the break-out that destroyed the German Army in Normandy.

The Battle of the Hedgerows was fought in the *bocage* country of the western region of Lower Normandy. The hedgerows formed a natural fortification network that facilitated the German defense.

THE STRATEGIC SITUATION

At the beginning of July 1944, the Allied lodgment area was far smaller than anticipated in the original *Overlord* plans. Three weeks after D-Day, Gen. Omar Bradley's First US Army had captured the port of Cherbourg, its initial tactical objective (for more information see Steven Zaloga, *Cherbourg 1944: The First Allied Victory in Normandy*, Osprey Campaign 278 (2015). In the British Second Army sector, the vital road junction of Caen had not yet been secured. This was in no small measure due to the balance of opposing forces in Lower Normandy.

From the German perspective, the British Second Army posed the greatest threat of a break-out from Normandy. The terrain beyond Caen was much more favorable for a mechanized advance to the Seine River and on to Paris. The terrain southeast of Caen was open farmland, well suited to tank operations. This was reflected in the Allied order of battle, with a preponderance of Allied tank strength in the British sector.

The British difficulties in breaking the German cordon was due in large measure to the density of opposing forces. By the middle of June, the British Second Army around Caen was facing four German Panzer divisions, with a combined strength of more than 675 German tanks and AFVs on a front only 20 miles wide. By way of comparison, the Wehrmacht's Herresgruppe Mitte (Army Group Center), the target of the Red Army's Operation *Bagration* offensive in late June 1944, had about 500 tanks and AFVs on a sector about 250 miles wide. In other words,

The British Second Army had a tough slog in the open country south of Caen due to the density of German defenses. Repeated tank attacks failed to breakthrough to the Seine River as originally planned. This is a pair of Canadian Sherman Fireflies of the Sherbrooke Fusilier Regiment knocked out in the fighting with the 12. SS-Panzer-Division "Hitlerjugend" on June 7, 1944.

Montgomery's forces were facing an opponent with an armored density about 15 times greater than the key summer battle fought by the Red Army. Even Herresgruppe Nordukraine, the most heavily defended sector of the Russian Front in June 1944, had a German armor density that was less than six times as dense as the German Panzer force facing the British in late June 1944.

The First US Army sector was further west than the British Second Army, and so more remote from the Seine River and Paris. Furthermore, the terrain was not well suited to mechanized operations. The terrain at the base of the Cotentin peninsula was tightly compartmentalized by *bocage*, the French term for coastal hedgerows. This situation was exacerbated by the sodden marshlands feeding into the Vire River estuary and numerous other rivers in the area. These marshlands were swollen by late June rain and some of the areas had been dammed and flooded by the German army to repel Allied airborne landings. The conditions in the bocage country were well known to the Heeresgruppe B commander, GFM Erwin Rommel, who had fought in the area during the 1940 Battle of France. The Germans recognized the defensive advantages of the *bocage* country, and so concentrated their limited forces, especially their premier Panzer divisions, in the British sector. The fighting in the *bocage* country was conducted primarily by infantry forces on both sides.

The British and Canadian attacks near Caen were frustrated by the opposition of concentrated Panzer forces as well as extensive anti-tank defenses. This is a 75mm PaK 40 anti-tank gun of the 12. SS-Panzer-Division "Hitlerjugend" south of Caen in June 1944.

CHRONOLOGY

June 6   D-Day invasion of Normandy.

June 23   Red Army stages Operation *Bagration* offensive.

June 24–30   Port of Cherbourg captured by VII Corps, First US Army.

June 29   Panzergruppe West starts a doomed counter-offensive against British forces near Caen.

July 3   Start of Battle of the Hedgerows by Middleton's VIII Corps.

July 4   Start of the Battle of the Hedgerows by Collins' VII Corps.

July 7   Start of the Battle of the Hedgerows by Corlett's XIX Corps.

July 7   30th Division secures bridgehead over the Vire River.

July 11   Panzer-Lehr-Division begins counter-attack of the Vire River bridgehead.

July 15   Start of final attacks on St Lô.

July 18   US forces enter St Lô.

July 19   St Lô cleared of German stragglers.

OPPOSING COMMANDERS

GERMAN COMMANDERS

As Germany's fortunes declined, Adolf Hitler played an increasingly intrusive role in directing military operations. By 1944 he gave his senior commanders very little discretion, even in minor tactical matters. This is very evident when German war planning is examined.

By the end of June 1944, Hitler had become disenchanted with the senior commanders in France and began wholesale changes. Oberbefehlshaber West (OB West: High Command West) was commanded through June 1944 by **Generalfeldmarschall Gerd von Rundstedt**. This theater command controlled two army groups in France, Heeresgruppe B on the invasion front in northern France and Heeresgruppe G in central and southern France. Hitler was displeased with the fall of Cherbourg and the failure of OB West to stage an effective Panzer counter-offensive in June 1944. Rundstedt was sacked on July 2, 1944 after complaining to the chief of the Wehrmacht high command, GFM Wilhelm Keitel, that he did not feel up to the increased demands being placed on him. He was replaced by **Günther von Kluge**, a favorite of Hitler for his leadership of the 4. Armee during the envelopment of the French armies through the Ardennes in 1940. Kluge had a distinguished record on the eastern front but was seriously injured in an automobile accident in October 1943. He was nicknamed "Clever Hans" for his political opportunism and vacillation. Like many Russian Front commanders, he arrived in France expecting to clean house of all the indolent slackers who had grown fat and lazy during the soft years of French occupation. He was shocked to discover the catastrophic tactical situation on the Normandy front. Kluge was aware of early plots against Hitler, and was privy to the July 20, 1944 plot. His leadership of OB West was short-lived. When the bomb plot against Hitler failed, the Gestapo was soon prying into Kluge's connection with the plotters. After the Normandy front collapsed in late July 1944, he realized his days were numbered. Expecting to be arrested, Kluge committed suicide on August 18. He was replaced by Hitler's miracle worker, the ruthless Walter Model.

Generalfeldmarschall Günther Hans von Kluge took over command of OB West in early July and subsequently took over Rommel's Heeresgruppe B command on July 17 after he was wounded in a strafing attack.

Generalfeldmarschall Erwin Rommel led Heeresgruppe B that controlled the two field armies in Normandy.

General der Waffen-SS Paul Hausser commanded the 7. Armee in Normandy after Gen. Dollman's death.

Generalfeldmarschall **Erwin Rommel** was assigned to command Heeresgruppe B on the invasion front in the autumn of 1943. Rommel considerably invigorated the defense effort, and put his own stamp on the Normandy tactics. He had studied the Allied landings at Sicily and Anzio, and was convinced that if the Allied bridgeheads could not be immediately crushed within a few days of landings, the weight of Allied naval bombardment and air power would ensure their survival. Rommel was wounded by a Spitfire strafing attack while visiting forward headquarters on July 17, and he would eventually become caught up in the witch-hunt for the July 20 plotters. Kluge took over the combined OB West/Heeresgruppe B leadership.

The 7. Armee (AOK 7) originally was commanded by **Generaloberst Frederich Dollman**. Through the end of June 1944, this field army controlled the French coast from the mouth of the Loire near St Nazaire, though Brittany and Normandy, all the way to the Pas-de-Calais. Dollman died of a heart attack on June 28. Rundstedt and Rommel both recommended that he be replaced by the 1. Armee commander, General der Infanterie Kurt von der Chevallerie, headquartered at the time in Bordeaux on the Atlantic coast. However, Hitler's growing disdain for the army commanders in France led him to appoint a Russian Front veteran, **General der Waffen-SS Paul Hausser**. Hausser was a professional soldier who had earned the Iron Cross in World War I and retired from the Reichswehr in 1932 as a lieutenant-general. He became involved in Nazi party politics and, because of his past military background, he was involved in the formation and training of the early Waffen-SS formations. So he was sometimes called "the father of the Waffen-SS." He led II SS-Panzer-Korps on the Russian Front in 1943 where he was wounded, losing an eye. By 1944, he was 64, 13 years older than his American opponent, Omar Bradley.

The forces under 7. Armee expanded through June 1944 and so there were originally plans to expand the field army to an Armeeabteilung. Instead, Panzergruppe West, under **General der Panzertruppe Leo Geyr von Schweppenburg**, was taken from 7. Armee's control and made into an independent command, later becoming 5. Panzerarmee. After having made critical remarks about Hitler's leadership, Geyr was relieved on July 4 and replaced by **General der Panzertruppe Heinrich Eberbach**. As a result, the sector directed by 7. Armee roughly corresponded with the American sector in Normandy while the Panzergruppe West command corresponded to the British/Canadian sector in the Caen area.

The two corps in Normandy under Hausser's 7. Armee were the 84 AK (LXXXIV Armee Korps) under **General Dietrich von Choltitz** and II Fallschirmjäger Korps under Luftwaffe **General Eugen Meindl**. Choltitz had begun the war in the Polish campaign as an infantry battalion commander, rising to divisional commander in August 1942 and to corps command in December 1942. He had won

the Knight's Cross for his battalion's performance in France in 1940. He would receive more attention later in the summer when he led the ill-fated and half-hearted defense of Paris. Meindl was a paratroop officer, and took corps command largely due to the important role of Luftwaffe paratroop divisions in this sector. Meindl had been an artillery officer in World War I, serving in mountain artillery at the outbreak of World War II. He switched from the Heer to the Luftwaffe paratroop force in 1940, and had his first combat jump in the 1940 landing at Narvik. His unit took part in the costly landings at Crete in 1942. He was decorated with the Knight's Cross and his skilled leadership led to his appointment as a Luftwaffe corps commander in November 1943.

ALLIED COMMANDERS

General Dwight Eisenhower led the Supreme Headquarters Allied Expeditionary Force (SHAEF), at the time based in Britain. Command of the Allied land forces in France was under **Field Marshal Bernard L. Montgomery**, commander of the 21st Army Group. During the initial fighting in Normandy, this consisted of two field armies, the First US Army and the British Second Army. It gradually expanded with the addition of the First Canadian Army and Patton's Third US Army. In early August, it split into Bradley's 12th Army Group controlling the US field armies and Montgomery's 21st Army Group controlling the British and Canadian field armies. Although there would be considerable tension between Montgomery and Bradley later in 1944, there were far fewer controversies in June–July 1944 regarding tactical options.

Bradley had been a classmate of Eisenhower's at the US Military Academy at West Point in the class of 1915. Like Eisenhower, he had not served in combat during World War I, though he had served in the Mexican Border War in 1916–17. George C. Marshall, the army chief of staff in World War II, had noted Bradley's superior performance while an instructor at the infantry

school in the early 1930s, and again while working on the General Staff in 1938 which accelerated his army career in later years. After raising the 82nd Division, Bradley served as deputy commander of II Corps under Gen. George S. Patton in North Africa in 1943. In Sicily, Bradley served as a corps commander, again under Patton's command. Bradley and Patton had known each other from the 1920s when they had both served in Hawaii. They were a complete contrast in style and temperament: Bradley, the son of a poor Missouri sodbuster, and Patton, from a wealthy California family with a long military tradition. While Patton's star waned after Sicily, Bradley's rose. Patton's decline began with an incident on Sicily where he slapped some shell-shocked soldiers for cowardice. Eisenhower had found Patton to be impetuous and difficult to control during his command of Seventh Army on Sicily. Bradley, in contrast, had proven himself to be an able and competent corps commander, if not so bold as Patton. After further impolitic outbursts to the press in England, Patton's career went into hibernation, making Bradley the choice to lead in France.

In July 1944, the First US Army in Normandy had four superior corps commanders. V Corps was commanded by **Maj. Gen. Leonard Gerow.** He served in the Mexican punitive expedition and again in World War I. He graduated first from the 1925 class at the Infantry School Advanced Course; Bradley graduated second. Eisenhower was his subordinate in the War Plans section immediately before the war. Gerow led V Corps during the D-Day landings on Omaha Beach. The neighboring XIX Corps arrived after D-Day and was commanded by **Charles H. Corlett,** one of two Pacific Theater commanders brought back to Europe to impart their experience; the other was VII Corps commander **Maj. Gen. J. Lawton Collins.** "Cowboy Pete" Corlett led the Kiska Task Force in 1942 that was assigned to take back the Aleutian Islands in Alaska from the Japanese. He then led the 7th Division in the invasion of Kwajalein in February 1944. He found the British and American *Overlord* planners to be insular and unwilling to listen to his advice about amphibious operations. The European Theater had conducted extensive amphibious landings in the Mediterranean but had never faced a seriously contested landing; Corlett realized that their D-Day landing plans paid insufficient attention to German defenses. He led XIX Corps through the Normandy campaign, but was relieved for medical reasons in October 1944. He was later assigned to lead a corps in the planned invasion of Japan in

1945. "Lightning Joe" Collins, the VII Corps commander, had commanded an infantry division during the fighting on Guadalcanal. Collins' corps had been responsible for the first major US victory in Normandy, the capture of Cherbourg in late June 1944. The VIII Corps commander, **Maj. Gen. Troy Middleton** had enlisted in the army in 1910 and had risen to regimental command in World War I. He had served as a divisional commander in Sicily and Italy before being given corps command.

SHAEF commander Gen. Dwight Eisenhower decorates VII Corps commander Maj. Gen. "Lightning Joe" Collins with the Distinguished Service Medal on July 21, 1944 while V Corps commander Maj. Gen. Leonard Gerow looks on. Collins received his nickname from his radio call sign while commanding an infantry division on Guadalcanal in 1943. A few days later, his corps played the central role in the Operation *Cobra* break-out.

XIX Corps commander Maj. Gen. Charles "Cowboy Pete" Corlett (left) and 30th Division commander Maj. Gen. Leland S. Hobbs (right) seen in Britain in May 1944.

OPPOSING ARMIES

THE GERMAN 7. ARMEE

The Germany Army did not anticipate the scale of losses suffered in the West in June 1944, and so replacements fell far short of needs. The army high command had anticipated 90,000 casualties on all fronts in June 1944, but in fact suffered over 165,000. The units in the west under OKW command estimated their June losses as 69,628, with 35,454 in France and the remainder in Italy and the Balkans. However, these estimates proved too low as losses in the Cherbourg campaign alone were about 55,000 men including Kriegsmarine and Luftwaffe, and the overall total in the West more than 83,000.

OKW was allotted only 34,500 replacements for these losses which had to be shared between OB West and the Italian Theater. By mid-July, OB West had been allotted 12,000 replacements of which only half had arrived. Total OB West casualties between D-Day and July 15 was about 100,000 men, roughly equivalent to all the infantrymen on the front lines on July 1. The dynamics of battlefield attrition were running strongly against the German defenders in Normandy. By early July, Heeresgruppe B recommended a switch to the "pipe-line" style of replacements used by the US Army, but it was too late to implement such a change. The unanticipated scale of casualties convinced Rundstedt that instead of three replacement battalions per division per month, at least ten per month were needed, nearly equivalent to the entire division's combat strength.

By the end of June 1944, OB West's logistics network was near to failure. Allied air strikes had caused the loss of the 10,050 tons of munitions, 1.6 million gallons (6.2 million liters) of fuel and lubricants, and trucks with the capacity for hauling 3,400 tons. By the end of June, units in OB West were suffering from a daily deficit of 220,000 gallons (833,000 liters) of fuel. The units had a daily requirement of 14,000 tons of truck capacity but had only about 5,000 tons. The French railway network was on the verge of collapse and on June 24–25, Allied air attacks shut down the last rail lines between France and

Manpower shortages in the Wehrmacht in Normandy led to desperate measures including the use of several Ost-Bataillon in Kampfgruppe König on the approaches to La Haye-du-Puits. These were made up of former Soviet soldiers who volunteered for the Wehrmacht to escape confinement in Germany's lethal prisoner-of-war stockades. The Eastern battalions in Normandy included Soviet troops from the far-flung republics including Volga Tartars and Georgians. These prisoners were photographed in a holding area near Bréhel in early August 1944.

The tank element of the 17. SS-Panzergrenadier-Division, SS-Panzer.Abt. 17, was equipped with 42 StuG IV assault guns as an expedient due to a shortage of normal tanks. It was similar to the more common StuG III, but based on the PzKpfw IV chassis. The battalion had been reduced to 11 operational StuG IVs when the US offensive resumed on July 3, 1944. This one was lost in the days preceding the start of Operation *Cobra*.

Germany. By the end of the month, OB West could only transport about 400 tons out of the daily minimum requirements for 2,250 tons of supplies (1,000 tons of munitions; 1,000 tons of fuel; 250 tons of rations).

Due to manpower sustainment problems in 1944, the German Army began to adopt different reporting practices regarding divisional strength and this became formal practice in April 1944. The previous practice of reporting overall strength (*Istbestand*) could be deceptive after divisions had suffered heavy casualties. For example, a division reporting a strength of 4,000 men might seem capable of combat but, in fact, the 4,000 men could be 3,800 men in non-combat roles such as administration and supply and only 200 men fit for combat duty. The most essential evaluation of the division, the "combat strength," only counted those troops actually involved in direct combat and they represented about 40–50 percent of overall strength in a full-strength unit. Since units in combat frequently did not have precise counts of troops, infantry divisions would report on their combat battalions in five states: strong (over 400 combat effectives); medium strong (over 300); average (over 200); weak (over 100); and exhausted (under 100 men). Likewise, corps reports to the field army headquarters were abbreviated to four levels of combat value for its divisions: (*Kampfwert*) 1 (suitable for offensive action); 2 (limited suitability for offensive action); 3 (suitable for defense); and 4 (limited suitability for defense).

Due to Hitler's perceptions of the Allied threat, Panzergruppe West contained the bulk of German forces in Normandy, and especially the more valuable units, with four corps in Normandy compared to two corps in the 7. Armee's Normandy sector. Apart from the 17. SS-Panzergrenadier-Division, all the Panzer and Panzergrenadier divisions in June 1944 were in the British sector, as well as all three of the heavy Nebelwerfer rocket artillery brigades.

In general, the 7. Armee was very weak in armor support, limited to divisional *Panzerjäger* companies and a few corps-level assault gun battalions. This was not widely regarded as a problem, since the local commanders

The most advanced small arm to see use in the hedgerow fighting was the FG 42 automatic rifle. This was a Luftwaffe weapon developed after the Crete airborne operation to provide the Fallschirmjäger with a compact weapon with high firepower. Although a popular and successful weapon, it was complicated and expensive to manufacture. This is an example captured during the St Lô fighting from II FS-Korps troops.

did not feel that the hedgerow terrain was at all conducive to tank or assault gun use. In fact, local German commanders were surprised at how extensively the Americans used armor, and how effective it was in certain circumstances.

The field artillery of 7. Armee was outgunned in terms of the quantity and quality of cannon. During the first week of July 1944, 7. Armee had about 350 guns and howitzers in its field artillery battalions compared to about 1,200 in the First US Army. Aside from the disparity in numbers, the German arsenal was an incredibly motley selection numbering 19 different types of which only half, about 190 guns, were the standard 105mm lFH 18/40 and 150mm sFH 18 divisional guns. The rest were expedient types including over 110 war-booty Soviet, French, and Italian guns. II Fallschirmjäger Korps was particularly weak in artillery and at the beginning of July three field artillery battalions were in the process of being transferred from the 19. Armee in southern France, equipped with war-booty Italian 149mm sFH 404(i) guns.

Ammunition supplies were not as lavish as in the First US Army. The ammunition issue (*Munitions-ausstattung*) for the standard 105mm lFH 18/40 was 125 rounds, based on expected expenditure in one day of heavy combat, and the division nominally had three issues per gun. At the start of the American offensive on July 3, 84. Korps had only about 180 rounds per 105mm howitzer, half a standard issue, while II Fallschirmjäger Korps had about 330 rounds per gun (88 percent); there was a re-supply of a further 560 rounds per gun in army-level depots. Overall, ammunition supplies had fallen from D-Day when there were about eight days of ammunition for the 105mm lFH 18, to less than three days' supply at the beginning of July 1944. It was somewhat better in the medium battalions, with levels having fallen from about seven days' supply on D-Day to about five in early July. Had the 7. Armee been able to use all their stockpiles in the July fighting, the exchange ratio against the US Army would not have been so bad and roughly on the order of 4:7 in favor of the Americans. Most of the OB West ammunition dumps were well behind the lines and subject to direct Allied air attack, and the truck and rail transport to the front was vulnerable to Allied air interdiction. The ammunition supply issue was further complicated by the need to supply some 11 different types of ammunition for the 19 different types of field guns and howitzers.

Although detailed artillery ammunition expenditure data for the 7. Armee sector is lacking, German artillery officers estimated that during July 1–10 fighting around Caen, Panzergruppe West had an artillery fire-exchange rate of 1:7.7 with the British/Canadian forces. The fire-exchange rate in the 7. Armee St Lô sector was no better since the Panzergruppe West sector was favored for heavy artillery. The 7. Armee estimated that in the week after the renewed American July 3 offensive, that First US Army was firing five to ten times as many rounds per day. Further examples are found in divisional records. On July 13, 1944, the 352. Infanterie-Division fired 2,200 rounds compared to 12,000 rounds from the attacking US 35th Infantry Division. During the final two days of fighting around St Lô on

July 17–18, the 352. Infanterie-Division fired 1,800 rounds versus 32,000 rounds from the US side. The imbalance late in the campaign was due to both a shortage of ammunition and a loss of cannons to American counter-battery fire. A First US Army report provided a critical assessment of the shortcomings of German field artillery in the Normandy fighting:

> The enemy did not employ his artillery to the full extent of its known capabilities. Hampered by very poor ground observation and no air observation or recent photo cover, the enemy largely fired map-data corrected on terrain features, road junctions, and bridges. This type of firing was sporadic and usually of a few rounds only. Although three observation units were located, their work could only be rated as mediocre. Counter-battery firing as well as the massing of fires were both the exception rather than the rule. There was no Corps artillery organization, with the limited available corps artillery usually either being attached to divisions without organic artillery or assigned a reinforcing role.

By July 1944, the German ground forces had given up any hope of air support from the Luftwaffe, and it was available only on a very limited basis. Fighter strength was being husbanded for strategic defense of the Reich, and bomber missions were mainly assigned to anti-ship operations against the Allied amphibious and transport fleet.

At the beginning of July 1944, 7. Armee had a combat strength of about 35,000 troops. 84 AK at the base of the Cotentin peninsula and on the east side of the Vire River contained the bulk of the 7. Armee units. The most critical sector at the base of the Cotentin was the western region bounded by the sea and the Gorges marshes. The US Army could have turned the flank of 84 AK in this sector in mid-June, but did not do so since the focus was on the capture of Cherbourg to the north. Hitler insisted that a defense line be established to block any future attempts. The initial outpost line was held by Kampfgruppe König, commanded by Eugen König who had led the 91. Luftlande-Division behind Utah Beach. All that was left of his division at the

Mortars were one of the most lethal infantry weapons in the *bocage* fighting. This is a German 81mm Granatwerfer 34.

The backbone of the German field artillery was the 105mm leichte Feld Haubitze 18, with three battalions in each infantry division. There were 129 of these in 7. Armee service in mid-July 1944, including some of the improved lFH 18/40 versions with the lightweight carriage.

start of July was about 400 combat effectives. Kampfgruppe König incorporated the left-overs from the units that had fought at the base of the Cotentin peninsula earlier in June during the Cherbourg campaign, including 2,600 men from the shattered 243. and 245. Infanterie-Divisions, plus 800 *Osttruppen*, former Red Army prisoners of war who volunteered to serve in the German Army. Since this formation stood in the way of the initial US offensive on July 3, it is worth describing in more detail.

The Kampfgruppe consisted of smaller formations, usually called *Untergruppen*, based around their previous formations. The chart below lists the sub-formations from west to east. Choltitz ordered the Volga-Tatar battalion withdrawn after one of its soldiers tried to shoot its German commander, but Simon's Untergruppe was so short of troops that the sullen ex-Red Army troops were left in place. Ost-Bataillon 635 under Oberst Bunjatchenko was also assigned to Kampfgruppe König, arriving shortly after the renewed American offensive on July 3. Even though König's force was short of infantry troops, a substantial amount of artillery remained from the original divisional formations. Armored support, aside from that of division Panzerjäger companies, included StuG.Abt. 902 with 30 StuG III assault guns and a few war-booty French light tanks from Panzer-Abteilung 100.

Kampfgruppe König, July 3, 1944

Untergruppe	Source	Combat Strength	Strength (battalions)
Eitner	265. Inf.Div.	1,000	2
Lewandowski	91. LL.Div.	400	2
Jäger	KG 265. Inf. Div. + Ost-Bataillon Huber	400+200	2
Simon	243. Inf. Div. + Tatar-Bataillon 627	1,200+600	3

Support weapons, Kampfgruppe König, July 3, 1944

75mm infantry gun	**12**
75mm PaK 40 AT gun	12
Soviet 76mm guns	34
88mm AT guns	6
105mm pack howitzer	2
Soviet 122mm guns and howitzers	14
150mm infantry howitzers	2
French light tanks	3
StuG III assault guns	35
Marder III tank-destroyers	9

A main line of resistance called the Mahlmann Line was established through the town of La Haye-du-Puits when the 353. Infanterie-Division was first stationed there in late June. It was followed by a secondary line 6 miles

The ammunition supply in German artillery units was complicated by the extensive use of war-booty weapons. This Soviet 122mm A-19 M1931 corps gun was probably from Batterie. 10, Artillerie-Regiment 265 that served with Kampfgruppe König in the fighting around La Haut-du-Puits.

(10km) further south called the Water Line (Wasserlinie) that followed the valleys of the Sèves and Ay rivers. Choltitz formed two further defense lines behind these, but they were seldom mentioned in official records because Berlin regarded rear defense lines as a sign of defeatism.

On the east side of the marshland was the 17. SS-Panzergrenadier-Division "Götz von Berlichingen." This division had seen small-scale combat since D-Day, originally in the Utah Beach area. In spite of its impressive designation, its armored element was made up of only 42 StuG IV assault guns and it had no armored half-tracks. It was motorized rather than mechanized, and it was short of trucks. The divisional reconnaissance battalion had been committed to the fighting near Carentan and bore the brunt of the division's 790 casualties in June. By the end of June, the division was still near full strength with a combat strength of over 6,000 men. It was reinforced by 1,200 men of the experienced but decimated Fallschirmjäger-Regiment 6 and a *Kampfgruppe* from the 275. Infanterie-Division. As a result, it was the strongest single division in the corps at the start of July 1944. It was reinforced by Panzerjäger-Abt. 657 which had 21 towed anti-tank guns in the 50mm–88mm range and five self-propelled Panzerjäger 4.7cm 35R (f).

Dollman had planned to pull this division out of the line at the end of the month to serve as the main 7. Armee reserve, and replace it with the newly arrived 353. Infanterie-Division. This was a full-strength division that had been stationed with the 7. Armee in Brittany and arrived in Normandy during the third week of June 1944. One of its regiments, GR 943, was immediately detached to reinforce the exhausted 352. Infanterie-Division near St Lô, yet the division still had significant strength at the start of July and was still in corps reserve behind the Mahlmann Line. The new 7. Armee commander, Paul Hausser, ordered it to begin moving east and it was still in transit on July 3 when the US offensive resumed. As a result, it was ordered to return to its original defense line to reinforce Kampfgruppe König. Parts of the division remained in corps reserve, while bits of the division were fed in as reinforcements through the July 1944 fighting. The other June reinforcement in the 84 AK sector was the 77. Infanterie-Division. This division left a portion of its divisional strength back at its home base in

St Malo and its contingent in Normandy had been beaten up in the Cotentin fighting in June and reduced to only about 2,000 combat effectives by the start of July 1944.

In late June 1944, the OKW began shifting the 2. SS-Panzer-Division "Das Reich" into Normandy from its original base in southern France, but not all elements had reached Normandy by the beginning of the month. Some of its units had been harassed by French partisans, leading to the infamous Oradour-sur-Glane massacre. It was kept in OKW reserve until July 2 when portions of the division were committed to reinforce Choltitz's corps.

II Fallschirmjäger-Korps near St Lô was significantly smaller than 84. AK, with only two divisions. In addition, the assigned corps support units, including FS-Artillerie-Rgt. 12 and FS-Flak-Rgt. 12, were not available at the beginning of July. II Fallschirmjäger-Korps had a single assault gun battalion, the Luftwaffe FS-StuG.Abt. 12 with an initial strength of 31 StuG III. The corps contained one of the best units in the American sector, the 3. Fallschirmjäger-Division. This was another 7. Armee asset that had been originally stationed in Brittany and then transferred to the St Lô sector in June. The division had been raised in 1944 and so had no combat experience prior to the Normandy fighting. However, it was based on well-motivated, volunteer troops who were put through strenuous training including jump training. In addition, the German paratrooper formations had an unusually high level of automatic weapons, giving them tactical firepower advantages. On the deficit side, the division had only a single artillery battalion available

One of the more obscure but effective anti-tank weapons used during the *bocage* fighting was the 88mm Raketenwerfer 43 Puppchen (Little Doll) rocket launcher. This weapon pre-dated the man-portable 88mm Panzerschreck and used a similar projectile, but with greater range. There were 130 of these in service with 7. Armee in 1944. This photograph of a captured example shows the electrically-initiated Panzerschreck round rather than the primer-fired Puppchen projectile.

in late June. Local German commanders considered this division to have the combat value of two regular infantry divisions, and its American opponents agreed. Its main tactical problem was that the lack of sufficient forces in its sector meant that it was overextended and all three regiments were deployed on the main-line-of-resistance (Hauptstellung) instead of the preferred tactic of keeping one regiment back in reserve.

7. Armee In Normandy, July 1, 1944

Unit	Commander	Combat strength
OKW Reserve		
2. SS-Panzer-Division	Gruppenführer Heinz Lammerding	5,000
Fallschirmjäger-Regiment 15	Oberst Kurt Gröschke	2,500
7. Armee	**Gen. der WSS Paul Hausser**	
84. Armee Korps	**Gen. der Inf. Dietrich von Choltitz**	
Kampfgruppe König	Gen.Lt. Eugen König	3,800
17. SS-Panzergrenadier-Division	SS-Brigadeführer Otto Baum	8,600
353. Infanterie-Division	Gen.Lt. Erich Müller	8,000
77. Infanterie-Division	Oberst Rudolf Bacherer	2,000
II Fallschirmjager-Korps	**Gen. der Flieger Eugen Meindl**	
3. Fallschirmjäger-Division	Gen.Lt. Richard Schimpf	10,000
352. Infanterie-Division	Gen.Lt. Dietrich Kraiss	6,000

The other division in II Fallschirmjäger-Korps was the 352. Infanterie-Division. This unit started the campaign in the Omaha Beach sector and was slightly over-strength on D-Day. However, during the subsequent fighting from June 6 to 24 it suffered casualties of 5,407, in effect its entire combat strength. By July 11, the division had suffered 7,886 casualties. The intention had been to pull it out of the line on June 15 and transfer it to southern France to be rebuilt. This was impossible due to the shortage of infantry divisions in Normandy. Its four replacement battalions, equivalent to only a third of the needed replacements, arrived in Montpelier in early July but were diverted to the defense of southern France. Another scheme to pull the division back into the Netherlands in early July also had to be abandoned due to the lack of a replacement unit. At the beginning of July 1944, the division had been reduced to a combat strength of about 2,000 men, consolidated into one of its three original regiments. To keep it in the line, it was reinforced by battle groups taken from the remnants of other infantry divisions. As a result, at the end of June it had a combat strength of 5,480 men, as detailed below.

Unit	Origins	Combat strength
KG Goth	GR 916, 352. ID	2,000
KG Kentner	GR 897, 266. ID	1,800
KG Böhm	GR 943, 353. ID	980
Reserve I	Schnelle-Brigade 30	200
Reserve II	II./GR 898, 343. ID	500
Total		5,480

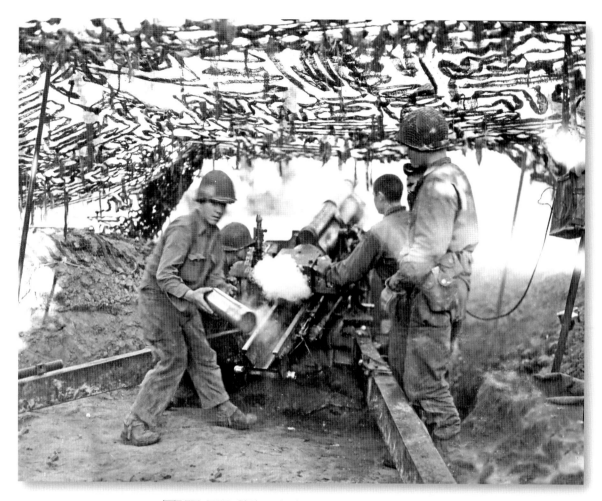

The workhorse of the US Army field artillery was the 105mm M2A1 howitzer with this one seen in action outside St Lô on July 18, 1944. Each infantry division had three battalions of these with 12 cannon each.

THE FIRST US ARMY

The First US Army in Normandy had four corps with 13 to 14 divisions facing two German corps with seven to eight divisions. Bradley's force was a bit large for an American field army since some of its elements were earmarked for Patton's forthcoming Third US Army.

The US infantry divisions in Normandy were uniform in composition and strength, but significantly different in combat experience and effectiveness. Several of the divisions had only recently taken part in the VII Corps offensive against Cherbourg. These four divisions (4, 9, 79, and 90) had suffered cumulative casualties of 12,665 in June, or an average of 3,165. They had been filled out with green replacements prior to the St Lô offensive. Divisions in the other corps varied in experience level with some divisions such as the 1st and 29th having fought since D-Day, while others were newly arrived and had not seen combat at the beginning of July. Although the divisions were usually well trained, fresh divisions thrown into the *bocage* fighting usually took days or weeks to become acclimatized to combat. In the case of the 30th Division, it was first put into the line in June in a quiet sector, and so gradually built up combat confidence before being thrown into the maelstrom of the *bocage*. Other units, such as the 83rd Division, were thrown into combat with no preparation, with predictable results.

Unit	Commander
First US Army	**General Omar N. Bradley**
VIII Corps	**Maj. Gen. Troy H. Middleton**
8th Infantry Division	Maj. Gen. Donald A. Stroh
79th Infantry Division	Maj. Gen. Ira T. Wyche
83rd Infantry Division	Maj. Gen. Robert C. Macon
90th Infantry Division	Maj. Gen. Eugene M. Landrum
VII Corps	**Maj. Gen. J. Lawton Collins**
4th Infantry Division	Maj. Gen. Raymond O. Barton
9th Infantry Division	Maj. Gen. Manton S. Eddy
XIX Corps	**Maj. Gen. Charles H. Corlett**
29th Infantry Division	Maj. Gen. Charles Gebhardt
30th Infantry Division	Maj. Gen. Leland S. Hobbs
35th Infantry Division	Maj. Gen. Paul W. Baade
3rd Armored Division	Maj. Gen. Leroy H. Watson
V Corps	**Maj. Gen. Leonard T. Gerow**
1st Infantry Division	Maj. Gen. Clarence R. Huebner
2nd Infantry Division	Maj. Gen. Walter M. Robertson
5th Infantry Division	Maj. Gen. Stafford L. Irwin
2nd Armored Division	Maj. Gen. Edward H. Brooks

Two armored divisions had arrived in Normandy by the beginning of July. The 2nd Armored Division was an experienced unit, having taken part in the Operation *Torch* landings in North Africa in November 1942, and having seen combat on Sicily in July 1943. The 3rd Armored Division was new to combat. US doctrine expected to use armored divisions for the exploitation mission once the infantry had broken through the enemy defenses. As a result, both armored divisions were being held back for an eventual offensive beyond the hedgerow country. Nevertheless, there were occasional uses of forces from these divisions during the St Lô campaign. The failure of Task Force Y of the 3rd Armored Division at Villiers Fossard on June 29–30 served to reaffirm the prudence of letting the infantry divisions conduct the breakthrough mission.

Through 1943, the US Army had overlooked the need for separate tank battalions to support the infantry divisions in their missions. This had become apparent during the Tunisian campaign in early 1943, leading to initial efforts to develop better combined-arms tank-infantry tactics. The September 1943 re-organization of the armored divisions freed up about 40 tank battalions and these provided almost enough to attach one tank battalion per infantry division in France in 1944. By mid-July 1944, the First US Army had a total of 11 separate tank battalions.

The US Army had established armored group headquarters to coordinate tank battalions at corps level rather than directly attaching them to divisions. This practice was still in place at the start of the Normandy campaign, but gradually gave way to a practice of semi-permanently attaching specific battalions to specific divisions once the advantages of

The heavy firepower of the divisional artillery was the 155mm M1 howitzer, with each infantry division having one battalion with 12 cannon. This is the 127th Field Artillery Battalion of the 35th Division in action north of St Lô on July 16, 1944.

having familiar units fighting alongside one another became clear. Due to the late change in US Army tank-infantry policy, its doctrine, training, and technology for tank-infantry cooperation were all a bit rough. The first field manual for tank infantry cooperation was not released until March 1944 and most divisions had little or no practical tank-infantry training prior to arriving in France. Neither the M4 medium tank nor the M5A1 light tank were well suited to the infantry support role, lacking the armor needed to resist typical German anti-tank weapons such as the 75mm PaK 40 anti-tank gun or Panzerschreck anti-tank rocket launcher. Although steps were underway to improve tank-infantry communication, the infantry platoon's SCR-536 "handie-talkie" was an AM transceiver that could not interact with the tank's FM radios; the company's SCR-300 "walkie-talkie" radio was FM, but operated on a different band to the tank radios. The shortcomings in doctrine, training, and technology were worked out during the course of the *bocage* fighting.

By mid-July 1944, First US Army had a total of 18 tank destroyer battalions of which 11 were equipped with the M10 self-propelled 3in. GMC and seven with the towed 3in. gun. Due to the lack of German armored vehicles in the *bocage* country, these battalions were used in other roles. The towed 3in. guns were unpopular in Normandy since they were too large and heavy to deploy in the *bocage*. More often, they were seconded to divisional artillery in an indirect fire role. The M10 3in. tank destroyers proved more useful and were generally deployed with the infantry divisions to provide mobile fire support as surrogate tanks.

The one area of unquestioned US Army superiority in Normandy was in field artillery. Artillery was the primary killing arm on the World War II battlefield, accounting for the majority of enemy casualties. US and German artillery composition at divisional level was similar on paper, with the

US infantry divisions having three 105mm howitzer battalions and one 155mm howitzer battalion. However, US units had their full equipment sets while German divisions in Normandy often had substitutes, such as war-booty weapons. US divisional artillery was more mobile than its German equivalent since it was fully motorized rather than horse drawn. In addition, it had a modern fire direction center networked downward to the infantry regiments and upward to corps artillery. Another important advantage was the addition of a pair of light aircraft for forward observation in each artillery battalion.

Aside from the field artillery advantages at divisional level, the First US Army enjoyed significant advantages at corps and field army level. Each corps generally had one or more field artillery groups, a headquarters controlling two to four field artillery battalions usually with 155mm howitzers or heavier weapons. The First US Army was supported by the 32nd Field Artillery Brigade, a special long-range formation which during this campaign usually had three 155mm gun and three 240mm howitzer battalions. These were used for interdiction and counter-battery missions. By the middle of July 1944, the First US Army and its subordinate corps had 51 non-divisional field artillery battalions including four 105mm towed howitzer, four 105mm self-propelled howitzer, three 4.5in. gun, 16 155mm howitzer, 11 155mm towed gun, four 155mm self-propelled gun, four 8in. howitzer, two 8in. gun and three 240mm howitzer battalions.

General Raymond Barton, commander of the 4th Infantry Division, bluntly described the importance of the field artillery during the Normandy fighting:

> The artillery was my strongest tool. Often it was my only reserve. My basic principle of artillery employment was to try to position it so that I could maneuver its fire in lieu of a maneuverable reserve. I repeatedly said that it was more a matter of the infantry supporting the artillery than the artillery supporting the infantry. This was an overstatement, but not too much of one. The basic evidence of that fact is that our doughboys never wanted to attack unless we could put a Cub (L-4) airplane in the air. I wish I knew the countless times that positions were taken or held due solely to TOT's. I also wish I knew the innumerable times, in some of which I personally participated, when [German] counterattacks were smeared by the artillery. And they were counterattacks that would have set us on our heels had it not been for the artillery.

TOT's were the acronym for "Time-on-target," also nicknamed "serenades." Field artillery is most lethal against infantry when the first rounds strike, and the number of casualties quickly diminish once the enemy escapes into fox-holes. Serenades were intended to increase the lethality of fire strikes by landing the first barrage on the enemy position simultaneously rather than in an erratic succession. The use of fire direction centers permitted US field artillery to conduct serenades at battalion, division or corps levels, massing multiple batteries or battalions.

Artillery ammunition stockpiles in the First US Army had not reached the desired levels by the beginning of July due to the Channel storm in late June that wrecked the artificial harbor at Omaha Beach. As a result, restrictions were applied for the July offensive with a corps-wide restriction to one unit-of-fire on the day of initial attack, half a unit-of-fire for a subsequent attack

For the German infantry in Normandy, the most hated and feared aircraft was the diminutive L-4H, a militarized version of the popular Piper Cub. These were used by the forward artillery observers of US Army field artillery battalions and their presence over German lines was usually followed by an artillery barrage. This particular aircraft was flown by 1Lt. John Donnelay of the V Corps artillery squadron.

and a third of a unit-of-fire on normal days. A unit-of-fire was the number of rounds of ammunition expected to be fired in a day of heavy combat. This varied by weapon; for example, it amounted to 120 rounds for the 105mm towed howitzer or 1,440 rounds per 105mm howitzer battalion. Even if artillery loads were below the usual standards, they were quite lavish compared to German supplies. During the two weeks of fighting up to the capture of St Lô, First US Army artillery use averaged half a unit-of-fire per day, as detailed in the chart below.

First US Army Field Artillery, July 1944

	Number of cannon			Ammunition expenditure			
	June 25	July 16	Daily in use	July 2–8	July 9–15	Daily avg.	Total
105mm howitzer	288+216*	468+234	524	170,710	328,600	35,665	499,310
155mm howitzer	204	324	294	79,597	116,053	13,975	195,650
155mm gun	60	108+48**	145	25,894	30,784	4,048	56,678
4.5in. gun	36	36	36	7,404	8,371	1,127	15,775
8in. howitzer	12	36	36	3,758	5,156	637	8,914
8in. gun		6	6	753	424	84	1,177
240mm howitzer		16	12	1,310	406	123	1,716
Total	816	1,276	1,053	289,426	489,794	55,658	779,220

* Towed 105mm howitzer + self-propelled M7 105mm HMC

** Towed 155mm gun + self-propelled M12 155mm GMC

OPPOSING PLANS

GERMAN PLANS

From the German perspective, the June fighting in Normandy had constricted the Wehrmacht's operational possibilities. In mid-June, Hitler had transferred another Panzer corps from the Russian Front to Normandy with the aim of staging a Panzer counter-offensive toward Bayeux to push the Allies into the sea. The relentless British pressure around Caen had forced the piecemeal commitment of Panzergruppe West and raised serious questions of whether there was any hope of eliminating the Allied beach-head. The field commanders, including Rommel and Rundstedt, made a sober appreciation of the situation and concluded that the Allied beach-head could no longer be eliminated but that at best it could be contained. Hitler continued to hold out hopes that a concentrated blow by the Panzer forces could have a decisive impact on the Normandy fighting, and he continued to dream up further schemes for such offensives.

The Wehrmacht was constrained in deploying further reinforcements to the Normandy front due to the limited forces available elsewhere in France and the Low Countries, the expectation of further Allied amphibious operations, and the consequences of the Soviet summer offensive. Hitler had already authorized the transfer of numerous divisions from Brittany and southern France to Normandy through the month of June 1944. He had refrained from a heavy drain of units out of the 15. Armee on the Channel coast due to the lingering belief that Patton's phantom "1st Army Group" was waiting in Britain to stage a second D-Day on the Pas-de-Calais. Berlin estimated that in July 1944 the Allies had a further 42 divisions stationed in Britain that could be landed somewhere in France. For German planners, Allied deception efforts combined with Allied naval supremacy in the Channel remained an alarming threat. Likewise, any excessive draw-downs of strength in Brittany or southern France would simply make these potential landing sites more attractive for an Allied amphibious landing.

The Red Army had launched Operation *Bagration* on June 23, 1944. Instead of striking northern Ukraine as expected by Berlin, the attack hit Heeresgruppe Mitte in Belarus. In five weeks of fighting, Heeresgruppe Mitte was largely destroyed, pushing the Red Army out of the Soviet Union and onto the flat plains of Poland in the direction of Warsaw and the Vistula River. In view of the massive losses during this fighting, it was no longer conceivable to reinforce the Normandy front from the Russian Front.

The constrained army resources left Hitler clutching at panaceas. At a June 17 meeting between Hitler, Wehrmacht chief-of-staff Jodl and the senior commanders in France, Hitler acknowledged that the balance of ground power on the Normandy front was shifting to the Allies. Until this could be rectified, Hitler insisted that the Kreigsmarine implement a vigorous mining campaign using new types of mines to interdict Allied shipping from Britain to Normandy. He also ordered the re-direction of the V-weapons against Allied debarkation ports, though this plan was abandoned shortly after the meeting. Hitler argued that a greater effort was needed by the Kriegsmarine and Luftwaffe until the army could mass enough forces for a major counter-offensive. By late June 1944, it was evident that these half-baked schemes were having no effect at all.

Through mid-June, Berlin had anticipated that Panzergruppe West would stage a major attack from Caumont toward Bayeux, splitting the American and British forces. In the face of Allied actions around Cherbourg and Caen, this plan was gradually abandoned. On June 24, Hitler changed his focus, promoting a scheme to strike against Carentan to split the American front and to relieve Cherbourg. Before any serious planning could be done, Cherbourg was encircled and British forces unleashed Operation *Martlet* near Caen, further delaying any hopes of a Panzer counter-offensive. The Allies maintained the operational initiative in Normandy.

Rommel and Rundstedt responded to Hitler's Carentan counter-attack scheme on 27 June, stating that German forces west of the Vire River were barely capable of holding current positions and in no state to stage a major counter-attack. The Panzer reserve that was in motion for a potential strike towards Bayeux, consisting of 1. SS, 9. SS, and 10. SS-Panzer Divisions, did not have the operational mobility to reach the base of the Cotentin peninsula due to the threat of Allied airpower. Hitler continued to press for an attack on Carentan, and Rundstedt responded on June 28 that such an attack could not begin at the earliest until July 10, and that he would prefer that the resources be directed against the greater British threat around Caen.

In view of the continuing British pressure, II SS-Panzer Korps began a counter-attack in the Caen sector at 1430hrs on June 29. The attack had a negligible impact. The following day, the commander of Panzergruppe West, Gen. Geyr von Schweppenberg, sent a caustic assessment of the situation demanding an end to the confusion at the senior command levels and a clear plan for future operations, not the current "tactical patchwork." Hitler did not take kindly to this veiled rebuke.

Amid these developments, Hitler held a major staff conference at Berchtesgarden on June 29, including Rundstedt and Rommel, as well as the navy and air force chiefs, Adm. Dönitz and GFM Göring. Although Hitler was determined to shift to the offensive in Normandy as soon as possible, he acknowledged the near term need to restrain the Allies in the Normandy bridgehead. The 7. Armee was to keep the Americans from advancing out of the constrictive *bocage* country while Panzergruppe West was to block any British advance beyond Caen toward Paris. Hitler argued that the situation could not be improved until Allied logistics were weakened by a combined Kriegsmarine mining campaign supported by Luftwaffe mine and torpedo attacks on Allied shipping in the Channel. By June 30, it became apparent that the II SS-Panzer Korps attack had utterly failed and that eventually Caen would have to be abandoned.

Hitler's decisions at the end of June 1944 tacitly accepted that the Wehrmacht had lost the operational and tactical initiative on the Normandy front. Germany's inability to stage a decisive counter-attack would force it to engage in an attritional struggle against the Allies. This was not a contest that favored Germany. The massive hemorrhage of Wehrmacht casualties on both the Normandy and Russian fronts in June 1944 left the Wehrmacht increasingly vulnerable to a catastrophic failure by mid-summer 1944.

ALLIED PLANS

In June 1944, the combat actions in Bradley's First US Army sector had been dominated by two principal operations. In the wake of the D-Day landings, the initial operation in the second week of June was the forging of a connection between the Omaha and Utah beach-heads by means of securing Carentan and the Vire River estuary located between them. This area was heavily fortified as Stutzpunkt Gruppe Vire (Strongpoint Group Vire) with substantial artillery support. Once this strongpoint was overcome, the focus shifted to the right flank, with the drive by Collins' VII Corps to cut off the Cotentin peninsula and then secure Cherbourg. This port city was of vital interest to Allied planners since it was badly needed to provide a logistics hub for Allied operations in Normandy. The capture of Cherbourg between June 26 and 30 set the stage for the next phase of First US Army operations.

On June 31, Field Marshal Bernard Montgomery, commander of the 21st Army Group, gave Bradley his mission for the month of July. The assignment was obvious and directed that First US Army would push through the *bocage* country south of the Cotentin peninsula and Omaha Beach to reach the line of Coutances–St Lô–Caumont. This would allow the First US Army to exit the most restricted areas of *bocage* into terrain more suitable for mobile operations. Once this objective had been met, the US contingent in Normandy would be expanded by the addition of Patton's Third US Army on the right flank near Coutances. Patton's forces would turn westward into Brittany to secure the ports at Quiberon Bay and Brest, while the First US Army would secure the right flank of the British/Canadian drive to the Seine River.

Bradley planned to start the offensive toward the south at the end of June, but it was delayed until early July due to the time needed to move Collins' VII Corps back from Cherbourg to the Carentan area. The First US Army deployment at the time was very uneven, with the left flank, east of the Vire River, much further south. The right wing, especially the units to the west of the Prairies Marécageuses de Gorges marshlands, were much further north of the objectives. At the same time, the right flank seemed to offer greater possibilities for a brisk advance since the German units facing the VII and VIII Corps there were mostly units that had been battered in the June fighting for Cherbourg and the Cotentin peninsula. The main opponent in front of VIII Corps, Kampfgruppe König, appeared to be little more than a grab-bag of left-overs from beaten units. Bradley decided to conduct the July offensive as a sequential operation starting with the corps in the west and moving east. He had hopes that a rapid advance could be made down along the coast, hopefully as far as Coutances, in the space of a few days. Bradley seriously underestimated the difficulties of conducting a campaign in the *bocage* country. The "Battle for the Hedgerows" was scheduled to start on Monday July 3, 1944.

THE CAMPAIGN

BOCAGE FIGHTING

Bocage is the Norman and French name for the style of terrain found in the western area of Basse Normandie (Lower Normandy) consisting of pastures boxed in by hedgerows. It is most common in the departments of Manche and Calvados west of the Orne River to the Cotentin peninsula, and so largely in the battle zone of the First US Army and German 7. Armee. The terrain east of the Orne gradually shifts to open pastureland and rolling hills where the British Second Army engaged Panzergruppe West.

An officer of the 329th Infantry described the hedgerows:

> These hard earthen banks, with their matted head-dress of stumpy trees and hedges, have been standing for centuries, as boundaries between tracts of land parceled out in the days of feudalism. As time went on, the land had been sub-divided in order to give each son a plot which he could call his own, until now the fields and orchards bordered by these hedgerows are so small that further

A good example of typical *bocage* country in Lower Normandy near the village of Saint-Hilaire-de-Briouze in the summer of 1944.

sub-division would render most of them useless for any form of farming or grazing. These hedgerows are fifty to one hundred yards apart, on the average, and made very formidable barriers to our advance, for the earthen portions range from three to eight feet in height and anywhere from three to ten feet in thickness at the base. From the tops of these banks grow the trees and hedges, thickened by the indiscriminate pruning carried on by the Norman farmers, who use them as a principal source of fire kindling wood.

The vegetation on top of the hedgerow provided concealment for the defenders and restricted the observation of the attacking force. *Bocage* complicated the use of field artillery since the vegetation could prematurely detonate the artillery rounds in the trees above before their intended impact against enemy positions. In addition, the hedgerows provided a solid basis for foxholes to shield against mortar and artillery fire.

From a military perspective, the hedgerows created a network of inverted trenches, forming a natural, layered fortification system that was well suited to defense. The earthen bases of the hedgerows shielded the defender from enemy fire and were thick enough to protect against small arms and machine-gun fire.

The Wehrmacht called the *bocage* fighting "*Buschkrieg*," Bush Warfare, a point clearly made by this photograph of a rifleman of the 79th Division in action near Lessay on July 18, 1944.

The *bocage* severely constrained maneuver by the infantry, and even more so for vehicles. Many hedgerows were too tall to be surmounted by tanks, and even the lower hedgerows created problems since a tank climbing over the earth wall exposed its weakly protected underside to enemy anti-tank weapons. The road network in the *bocage* was poor since this region did not

The US Army characterized the hedgerow as a "system of inverted trenches." Here, a rifleman of the 29th Division has created a firing embrasure by cutting an opening in the base of a hedgerow.

German *Bocage* Defense

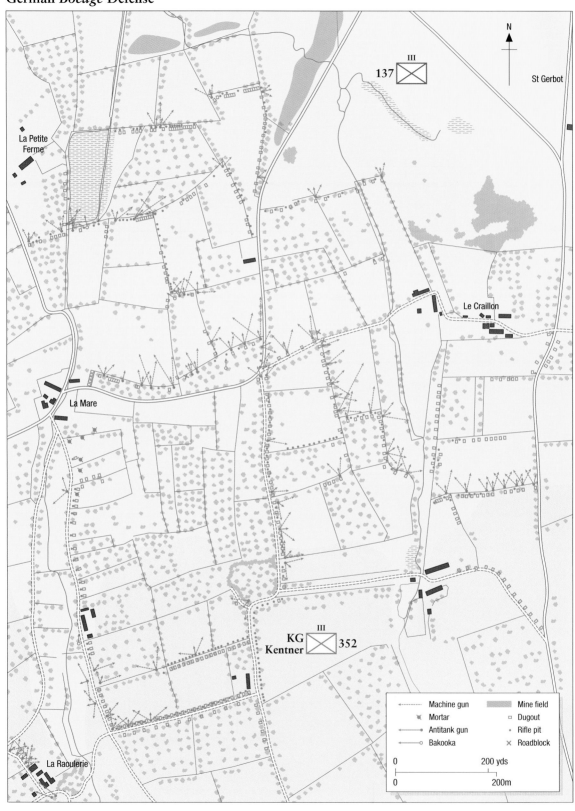

La Petite Ferme

St Gerbot

137 III

Le Craillon

La Mare

KG Kentner III 352

La Raoulerie

Machine gun		Mine field
Mortar		Dugout
Antitank gun		Rifle pit
Bakooka		Roadblock

0   200 yds

0   200m

make much use of motorized farming techniques. Aside from a limited number of regional roads between the major towns, the individual hedgerows were connected by small openings and footpaths with the occasional cart path or small unpaved road.

The *bocage* country was well suited to German defensive doctrine. The outer layer of the German defenses was a thinly manned outpost line. This served to identify the approach of American units and the tenacious defense of an outpost line by a small number of troops was often able to stop the advance of a much larger force. Furthermore, it served to tie down the attacking force, fixing it in place for mortar and artillery bombardment. In the event that the outpost line was captured, one or more additional defense lines were behind it to provide resilience. This type of defense was not entirely dissimilar to World War I trench warfare. However, there were some significant differences. The German commanders called this fighting "*Buschkrieg*," bush warfare. Static defense was not sufficient since the defense lines could be gradually worn down by infantry attack and artillery fire. German commanders placed considerable stress on the individual initiative of small unit commanders. Once the attacking force was halted by machine-gun and mortar fire at the outpost line, small combat teams would maneuver on foot to further disrupt the attack by strikes against their flank or rear.

An anonymous US Army officer provided a pungent and succinct description of hedgerow fighting techniques from the American perspective:

> There were just three ways that our infantry could get through the hedgerow country. They could walk down the road, which always makes the leading men feel practically naked (and they are). They could attempt to get through gaps in the corners of the hedgerows and crawl up along the row leading forward, or rush through in a group and spread out in the field beyond. This was not a popular method. In the first place often there were no gaps, just when you wanted one most. And in the second place, the Germans knew

OPPOSITE

This provides an example of typical German defense configurations in the *bocage* fighting. This area, between the village of La Meauffe and St Lô, was held by roughly a battalion of troops from Kampgruppe Kentner. This was a combat formation based on Grenadier-Regiment 897 of the 266. Infanterie-Division that was detached to the 352. Infanterie-Division in mid-June 1944. It suffered so many casualties during the July fighting that it was reinforced with II./GR 898 and II./GR 899. This sector was called the "La Mare–Le Carillon Nose" position by the attacking 35th Division since it formed a distinctive salient. The 2/137th Infantry pushed into the defenses on July 13–14, but the position was not finally cleared out until it was out-flanked to the southeast.

The size and density of the hedgerows varied. Here, a squad from the 175th Infantry, 29th Division dig their foxholes in the base of a hedgerow to the northeast of St Lô on July 15, 1944.

about the gaps before we did and were usually prepared with machine-gun and machine-pistol reception committees. The third method was to rush a skirmish line over a hedgerow and then across the field. This could have been a fair method if there had been no hedgerows.

Usually we could not get through the hedge without hacking a way through. This of course took time, and a German machine gun can fire a lot of rounds in a very short time. Sometimes the hedges themselves were not thick. But it still took time for the infantryman to climb up the bank and scramble over, during which time he was a luscious target, and when he got over the Germans knew exactly where he was. All in all it was very discouraging to the men who had to go first. Of course the Germans did not defend every hedgerow, but no one knew without stepping out into the spotlight which ones he did defend.

It was difficult to gain fire superiority when it was most needed. In the first place, machine guns were almost useless in the attack because about the only way they could be used was to fire from the hip. If you set them up before the advance started, they had no field of fire and could not shoot the enemy. If you carried them along until you met the enemy, still the only way to get them in position was to set them up on top of a hedgerow bank. That was not good because the German was in the next bank and got you before you set the gun down. Anyway, it had to be laid on the bank, no tripod, just a gun barrel lying unevenly on its stomach. On the other hand the Germans could dig their guns into the banks in advance, camouflage them, and be all set to cover the roads, trails, and other bottlenecks our men had to use.

The artillery was the major fire support weapon. But it suffered certain handicaps. In the first place it had to be adjusted from the front line by forward observers. These sometimes had difficulty knowing just where they were, and the trees frequently delayed adjustment because of the short vision. If you found the enemy in the next hedgerow he was frequently less than 100 yards from you, and that was too close for artillery fire, particularly since short rounds would probably burst in the trees over your men in your own hedgerow. If the enemy was two or more hedgerows ahead of you, that wasn't so good either, because the mere delay in getting to him through that last hedgerow just in front of him gave him time to rise up and smite you after the artillery lifted. The mortars were effective providing you knew just what to shoot at and where it was, but the infantryman still had the delay and exposure of getting through the last hedgerow.

The Germans, being on the defensive, profited by these minor items of the terrain. They could dig in, site their weapons to cover the approaches, and prepare tunnels and other covered exits for themselves. Then when our men appeared, laboriously working their way forward, the Germans could knock off the first one or two, cause the others to duck down behind the bank, and then call for their own mortar support. The German mortars were very, very efficient. By the time our men were ready to go after him, the German and his men and guns had obligingly retired to the next stop. If our men had rushed him instead of ducking down behind the bank, his machine gun or machine pistol would knock a number off. For our infantrymen, it was what you might call in baseball parlance, a fielder's choice. No man was very enthusiastic about it. But back in the dugout I have often heard the remark in tones of contempt and anger: "Why don't they get up and go?"

The tanks are no better off. They have two choices. They can go down the roads, which in this case were just mud lanes, often too narrow for a tank, often sunk four to six feet below the adjacent banks, and generally deep in mud. The Class 4 roads were decent in spots, but only for one-way traffic, with few exits to the adjacent fields. An armored outfit, whether it is a platoon

Both sides made extensive use of anti-tank rocket launchers as improvised artillery in the *bocage* fighting. This is a rifleman of the 79th Division using a 2.36in. bazooka M1A1 rocket launcher on July 18, 1944. From late June to late July 1944, US infantry fired nearly 53,000 bazooka rockets, mostly against targets other than tanks.

Light mortars were one of the most effective weapons in the *bocage* fighting. Each US Army rifle company had a weapons platoon that included three mortar squads, each with one 60mm M2 mortar.

or an armored army, attacking along a single road attacks on a front one tank wide. The rest of the tanks are just roadblocks trailing along behind. When the first tank runs into a mine or an 88 or 75 shell, it always stops, and it usually burns up. And it efficiently blocks the road so the majestic column of roaring tanks comes to an ignominious stop.

The next step is to try to find out where the enemy gun or tank is, and wheel up a tank or so to shoot at him. The only trouble is, only the men in the first tank saw the German's gun flash, and they aren't talking any more. The tanks trying to get into position to do some shooting are easily seen and get

One of the "lessons-learned" during the *bocage* fighting was it was safer to cross a field in the center than along a lateral hedgerow since the Germans invariably covered the corners with machine-gun positions. This is a squad of the 79th Division in action in the Lessay area on July 17.

The Wehrmacht deliberately flooded many areas of lower Normandy to complicate any attempts at airborne landings. In this case, the Séves River near Baupte, west of Carentan was dammed to flood the fields near the town's 16th-century church, Église Notre Dame.

shot before they can do much about it. I have seen it happen. In the hedgerows it is almost impossible to get firing positions in the front row, and in the rear you can't see the enemy anyway so no one bothers. Usually the tanks waited for the infantry to do something about it.

Instead of charging valiantly down the road, the tanks may try to bull their way through the hedgerows. This is very slow and gives the enemy time to get his tanks or guns where they can do the most good. Then he just waits. And in the solution, there is always a minor and local problem to be solved, a problem which caused a certain amount of irritation, and that is, who is going over the hedgerow first, the infantry or the tank? It is surprising how self-effacing most men can be in such situations.

Anyone who actually fought in the hedgerows realizes that, at best, the going was necessarily slow. A skillful, defending force could cause great delay and heavy losses to an attacking force many times stronger. This, because the attacker can't use his fire power effectively and because he can't advance rapidly except on the road where he is quickly stopped at some convenient spot.

There were a number of other factors which contributed to the difficulties of fighting through the hedgerows. The area was merely a succession of small enclosed pastures with a few orchards, likewise enclosed by hedgerows. Seldom could one see clearly beyond the confine of the field. It was difficult to keep physical contact with adjacent squads, platoons, or larger units. It was difficult to determine exactly where one was. Unlike conditions in open country, flanks could not be protected by fields of fire. All these contributed to the difficulties of control and caused a feeling of isolation on the part of small units. All this meant that the front-line troops thought their neighbors were nowhere around. They could not see them, they were not in the adjacent field, therefore they were behind. Often this feeling of being out on a limb would cause the leading elements to halt and wait for the flank units to come up (and sometimes these were ahead).

German counterattacks in the hedgerows failed largely for the same reasons our own advance was slowed. Any attack quickly loses its momentum, and then because of our artillery and fighter bombers the Germans would

BATTLING IN THE *BOCAGE* (PP. 38–39)

US infantry units received no specialized training for combat in the hedgerows prior to the Normandy campaign. This was partly due to the concentration on the elaborate preparations for the amphibious landings on D-Day. In addition, there were misconceptions about the Normandy hedgerows. There were extensive hedgerows on the opposite side of the Channel in the southern English countryside. However, the English hedgerows were not as substantial as their Norman counterparts.

Most infantry weapons were not well suited to hedgerow fighting. German defenses were dug into the earthen base of the hedgerows, making them far less vulnerable to rifle fire. Furthermore, the extensive vegetation on top of the earthen base provided excellent camouflage and helped conceal the precise location of the German defenses. Light machine guns provided a somewhat better solution, since their volume of fire provided better suppression than aimed rifle fire.

As the GIs became more experienced in hedgerow fighting, other types of weapons were preferred. One of the most common weapons used in the *bocage* fighting was the rifle grenade (1). These could be fired from the normal M1 Garand rifle using an adapter that was fitted to the barrel and launched using a special blank cartridge. The rifle grenade could be fired from the normal shoulder position. However, to get maximum range, the rifle was fired from a kneeling position with the butt firmly against the ground and the rifle elevated to a 45-degree angle, giving it an effective range of about 55 to 300 yards depending on whether an auxiliary booster cartridge was used. The range of the grenade could be adjusted by using five range rings on the grenade adapter that altered the speed of the grenade depending on how deep the grenade stabilizer tube was mounted on the adapter.

The M1A1 2.36in. "bazooka" rifle launcher was another popular weapon in the *bocage* fighting (2). These weapons were not widely distributed in the rifle companies, with only five per company. Once their value in *bocage* fighting became evident, many infantry divisions took the bazookas allotted to service units and headquarters units and transferred them to the rifle companies. Although intended primarily for anti-tank defense, their high explosive warhead was effective against dug-in defenses.

The US Army avoided using field artillery close to friendly troops. This was not only due to inherent problems of accuracy. The use of field artillery in the *bocage* was complicated by the possibilities of projectiles prematurely detonating over friendly troops if they came into contact with trees and overhead branches when fired on a shallow trajectory. As a result, the 60mm M2 light mortar became the workhorse of the infantry for close-range fire-support (3). This could fire a mortar bomb from 100 to 1,985 yards, enabling the weapon to cover the gap between the forward edge of battle and the inner limit of field artillery support. Each rifle company had three 60mm mortars.

One obvious solution to penetrating the hedgerows was the use of dozer tanks, like this one, "Apache" of Co. A, 70th Tank Battalion, attached to the 4th Infantry Division for most of the hedgerow campaign. However, this was a fairly new device and there were seldom enough of these to have an appreciable impact on the fighting. Each tank battalion was supposed to have four of these, but shortages as well as combat losses meant that this objective was seldom reached.

suffer disastrous loss. In fact we found that generally the best way to beat the Germans was to get them to counterattack – provided we had prepared to meet them.

Although the hedgerows were the most distinctive feature of the *bocage* region, the numerous rivers and marshes further aided the defense and impeded maneuver. The July 1944 fighting took place in the area dominated by the Vire and Taute rivers as well as associated rivers and streams. The numerous small rivers running through the coastal lowlands created several large marshes that further compartmentalized the terrain and made maneuver even more difficult. East of La Haye-du-Puits was the Marais-de-Ste.-Anne swamp, fed by the Séves River. Immediately south of Carentan was the Prairies Marécageuses de Gorges, a substantial marshland fed by the Taute River and many small tributaries. In the months prior to D-Day, the Wehrmacht flooded a number of areas by using dams or other obstructions in order to complicate any Allied attempts at airborne landings. The extent of these marshlands increased in late June 1944 since the early summer of 1944 was the rainiest on record since 1900.

THE VIII CORPS ADVANCE ON LA HAYE-DU-PUITS

The First US Army offensive began at 0530hrs on Monday, July 3 in Middleton's VIII Corps sector. Both the 79th and 90th Divisions had taken heavy losses in the Cherbourg/Cotentin campaign in June and both had about 40 percent replacements in their rifle companies. Wyche's 79th Division was regarded as the sounder of the two, and there had been a change in command in the 90th Division in hopes of improving its disappointing performance during the Cotentin peninsula fighting in June. The 82nd Airborne Division had already suffered about 50 percent casualties since D-Day and was

The Marshland Advance, July 3–11, 1944

A German infantry squad in Normandy during the summer of 1944. The third *Landser* is carrying one of the new Panzerfaust anti-tank rockets.

scheduled to be returned to Britain in a few days for rebuilding. In spite of its numerical weakness, it was regarded as the most effective force in the corps due to its superior leadership and troop performance. The weather was far from favorable on the first day, with a steady downpour that prevented air support and limited artillery observation.

The 82nd Airborne Division in the center of the advance made the best progress. A reinforced company of the 505th Parachute Infantry Regiment (PIR) infiltrated the German outpost line in the Bois d'Etenelin (Hill 113) from the north while the 508th PIR took the southwest side. Ost-Batallion Huber stationed along Kampfgruppe König's outpost line was overwhelmed before it realized that an attack had started. At first, Hausser's 7. Armee headquarters thought that the attack was simply a reconnaissance in force as it was presumed the Americans wouldn't attack in such poor weather; there had not been the usual pre-attack air sorties, and the rain and fog had obscured any observation of the American activity. By mid-morning, Hausser realized that a major attack was underway. The 353. Infanterie-Division, which had pulled out of the Mahlmann Line the day before to transfer further east, was ordered to turn around and return to its original defensive line.

A squad from Co. F, 2/359th Infantry of the 90th Division during the fighting for Mont Castre near St Jores on July 6, 1944. The rifleman in the center is preparing to fire a rifle grenade over the hedgerow.

The 82nd Airborne Division's main effort by the 325th Glider Infantry Regiment (GIR) was aimed at securing the ridgeline topped by the hamlet of La Poterie. This hamlet was in fact on the edge of the Mahlmann Line, the main-line-of-resistance (*Hauptstellung*). The first wave of reinforcements, Ost-Bataillon 635, intervened and the glider-infantry force also came under

GERMAN FRONT LINE, MORNING JULY 3, 1944

DUPINE RIDG

HILL 131

7

5

6

79 WYCHE

MAHLMANN LINE

LA HAYE-DU-PUITS

C

8

D

2

12

10

1

HILL 95

LA POTERIE RIDGE

E

353 MÜLLER

EVENTS

1. The 505th PIR crosses the start-line near Varenguebec at 0630hrs, July 3, with its 2nd and 1st Battalions in column. The 2/505th captures the Dupinerie ridge around 0830hrs.

2. The 508th PIR jumps off at 0630hrs with the 2/508th PIR on the right and 3/508th PIR on the left.

3. Ost-Bataillon Huber is largely overwhelmed by the 82nd Division assault and numerous troops surrender.

4. The 325th GIR jumps off at 0630hrs with 2/325th GIR on the right and 1/325th GIR on the left. The advance by the 325th GIR is held up by delays on their right (eastern) flank by the 90th Infantry Division. The regiment reached Faudemer around 1600hrs.

5. Untergruppe Lewandowski begins to pull back southward to the Mahlmann Line by late morning. Portions of the 353. Infanterie-Division begin returning to the Mahlmann Line during the day, re-establishing a secondary defense line.

6. The 2/508th PIR captures the southern slope of Hill 131 around 1145hrs and is joined by the 3/508th PIR around 1600hrs.

7. The 505th PIR captures the north side of Hill 131 around 1225hrs. The regiment is

instructed to take over control of the entire hill at 1550hrs to free up the 508th PIR to assist in the capture of La Poterie Ridge.

8. Elements of the 353. Infanterie-Division begin to return to the Mahlmann Line by late afternoon.

9. Strong resistance by the 353. Infanterie-Division along the Mahlmann Line delays the planned advance of the 325th GIR. Their objective is reduced to the capture of the village of La Poterie while the other elements of the division are assigned to assault the La Poterie Ridgeline.

10. The 1st and 3rd Battalions, 505th PIR launch an attack on the Mahlmann Line at Hill 95 around 0800hrs and secure the objective around 1150hrs. They meet up with the 314th Infantry, 79th Division to the west of the main road at 2100hrs.

11. The 508th PIR passes through the 505th PIR to reinforce the attack on La Poterie ridgeline. They reach the top of Hill 95, but a counter-attack by GR 943 pushes them off. The hill is recaptured around midnight.

12. The intense fighting around Hill 95 leads to the commitment of the divisional reserve, the 507th PIR which attacks the western hill starting at 2015hrs.

13. The 1st and 3rd Battalions of the 325th GIR attack the village of La Poterie at 0800hrs and secure the village by 1250hrs. The regiment is instructed to take up defensive positions and to establish contact with the 90th Division to the east.

82ND AIRBORNE DIVISION ATTACK TOWARDS
LA HAYE-DU-PUITS, JULY 3–4, 1944

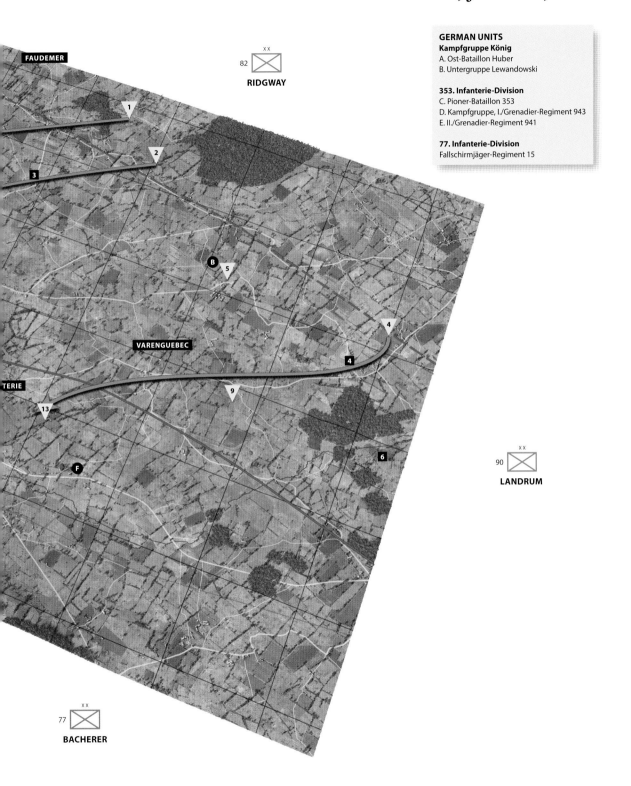

GERMAN UNITS
Kampfgruppe König
A. Ost-Bataillon Huber
B. Untergruppe Lewandowski

353. Infanterie-Division
C. Pioner-Bataillon 353
D. Kampfgruppe, I./Grenadier-Regiment 943
E. II./Grenadier-Regiment 941

77. Infanterie-Division
Fallschirmjäger-Regiment 15

FAUDEMER

82 ⊠ ××
RIDGWAY

VARENGUEBEC

TERIE

90 ⊠ ××
LANDRUM

77 ⊠ ××
BACHERER

A squad from the 90th Division advances cautiously along a ditch while under the protective watch of an M4 medium tank of Co. C, 712th Tank Battalion on July 7, 1944 near St Jores.

heavy artillery fire since it was in clear view of forward observers on Mont-Castre immediately to the south. When the initial attack was stopped, the 508th PIR was ordered to continue southward to help take the three hills from Ste Catherine (Hill 95) to La Poterie. The advance ground to a halt shortly before midnight as reinforcements arrived from the 353. Infanterie-Division. It took another two days of fighting to secure the hills due to the arrival of GR 941 of the 353. Infanterie-Division and accurate German artillery fire. By the afternoon of July 5, the 82nd Airborne Division took control of the three hilltops after advancing about 4 miles. The 82nd inflicted

The 79th Infantry Division finally liberated La Haye-du-Puits on July 8, 1944. This is an 81mm mortar team from the 315th Infantry, 79th Division entering the town on Rue de Barneville. The soldier in the right foreground is carrying the 81mm mortar tube while the soldiers behind carry the bipod and base-plate.

about 1,300 German casualties including 772 POWs. It remained in the area until July 7 when it was pulled out of the line and replaced by the 79th Division.

While the 82nd Airborne Division fought for the La Poterie Ridgeline, the 90th Division was assigned to take Mont Castre, one of the main strongpoints on the Mahlmann Line. The approach to the wooded hill was along a narrow corridor bordered on the west by the hill itself and to the east by the marshes of Prairies Marécageuses de Gorges. Dense *bocage* and thick woods on Mont Castre constricted this sector. An assault battalion of the 358th Infantry was halted by the German outpost line near the hamlet of Les Sablons and waited for artillery support before proceeding. After seeing a German assault gun and some half-tracks, the battalion called for tank destroyer support which further delayed the attack. Another battalion was pushed forward, but artillery support directed from Mont Castre frustrated the attack and the 90th Division advanced only about 3,000 yards at a cost of 600 casualties. The attack resumed very slowly on Tuesday, July 4 when the lead battalions went to ground after an artillery bombardment had convinced them that a German counter-attack was imminent. The artillery fire was not especially heavy, but it was very accurate due to the presence of German forward observers on the Mont Castre heights above. The advance finally began to pick up some momentum by late in the day, finally reaching the road to La Haye-du-Puits; casualties were heavier than the day before and numbered about 700. The 90th Division finally captured Mont Castre on Thursday, July 6, but its hold was tenuous. Hausser reinforced this sector and staged a counter-attack from the south side of Mont Castre on July 7 using III./SS-Panzergrenadier-Rgt. 3 from 2. SS-Panzer-Division "Das Reich" and a *Kampfgruppe* of the 77. Inf. Div. These attacks were pushed back with heavy losses on both sides. An attempt to push the 357th Infantry down the corridor east of Mont Castre was stopped short of the Canal du Plessis,

This is a scene in La Haye-du-Puits on July 9, 1944 as troops of the 12th Engineer Battalion, 8th Infantry Division pass through the shattered city.

An SdKfz 222 light armored car from 1./SS-Panzer Aufklärüngs-Abt. 17, knocked out during the fighting with 1/8th Infantry, 4th Infantry Division during the fighting south-west of Carentan on July 15, 1944.

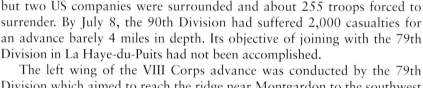

but two US companies were surrounded and about 255 troops forced to surrender. By July 8, the 90th Division had suffered 2,000 casualties for an advance barely 4 miles in depth. Its objective of joining with the 79th Division in La Haye-du-Puits had not been accomplished.

The left wing of the VIII Corps advance was conducted by the 79th Division which aimed to reach the ridge near Montgardon to the southwest of La Haye-du-Puits. At the start of the advance on July 3, the 314th Infantry attempted to seize Hill 121 on the left flank, part of the outpost line of a *Kampfgruppe* from the 243. Inf. Div. The hill was partially occupied on the first day of the attack but it took another day to clear the German defenders from small strongpoints around the hill. The hill offered excellent vantage points for artillery forward observers while at the same time denying the outposts to the Germans. The advance over the first two days through the *bocage* was slow but steady. The *Kampfgruppe* from the 243. Inf. Div. launched a serious counter-attack on the evening of July 4 during its attempts to withdraw from the outpost line to the main-line-of-resistance on the Montgardon Ridge. On the morning of the 5th, the 79th Division tried to make a rapid penetration of the German defenses by committing the reserve 313th Infantry, but before reaching its objective of the Ay River, the task force was hit with a heavy artillery barrage followed by a counter-attack that pushed the task force back to its start position. Although this advance had failed, the neighboring 315th Infantry with tank support reached the north slope of Hill 84, part of the

The 83rd Division conducted the VIII Corps advance on the left flank along the Taute River. Here, the divisional commander, Maj. Gen. Paul Baade, discusses plans with one of his staff officers, Capt. Smith.

Montgardon Ridgeline. Over the next two days, the 79th Division's three regiments fought a series of disconnected skirmishes in the *bocage* to secure Hill 84 and Montgardon itself.

The original VIII Corps plan had assumed that once La Haye-du-Puits was outflanked that the Germans would withdraw. Although US forces held both Mont Castre and Montgardon, the 7. Armee had no intention of withdrawing. A *Kampfgruppe* based around SS-Panzergrenadier-Rgt. 4 of the 2. SS-Panzer-Division had arrived in this sector on July 4 and reinforced the existing defenses along the Mahlmann Line. On the afternoon of 7 July, a *Kampfgruppe* under Sturmbannfuhrer Otto Weidinger hit the defense line on Montgarden and nearly pushed it off the ridgeline before being repulsed after the loss of three tanks.

Although the VIII Corps offensive had pushed through the Mahlmann Line after five days of fighting, the operation had fallen far short of its objectives. Bradley's expectation that the 84. AK would withdraw after a hard push proved to be fundamentally mistaken. The five days of fighting cost both American divisions 2,000 casualties each and neither division was in any position for further offensive action in view of the heavy losses suffered in June during the Cherbourg fighting. Some 1,482 Wehrmacht troops had been captured, but these were mainly *Osttruppen*. La Haye-du-Puits finally fell on July 9 to the 79th Division. VIII Corps resumed its attack during the second week of July, and finally came up along the Ay River by July 14. It took 12 days of fighting to advance 12,000 yards.

Although VIII Corps had failed in its tactical objectives, it had important operational consequences for the First US Army. Hausser's plan to use the 353. Infanterie-Division to permit a shift of the 17. SS-Panzergrenadier-Division back into the corps reserve had been prevented. Not only was one of the two army mechanized formations tied down on the front line, but the weakness of the 84. AK sector had also forced Hausser to begin committing elements of his other mechanized reserve, the 2. SS-Panzer-Division. Removing the mechanized forces from the 7. Armee reserve would prove lethal to the German defenses two weeks later.

THE VII CORPS ADVANCE FROM CARENTAN

Collins' VII Corps started its advance a day after the neighboring VIII Corps on Tuesday, July 4, 1944, pushing out of Carentan. Its task was unenviable. On its left (western) flank was the Prairies Marécageuses de Gorges swamps. On its right (eastern) flank was the rain-swollen Taute River. In between was a dry isthmus only 2 to 3 miles wide that was congested with *bocage*. There was no maneuver room. This meant that only a single division could be committed to this front until the corps reached the more open ground in the vicinity of the Périers–St Lô road. Collins planned to use the fresh but inexperienced 83rd Division for this mission. Facing them was a regiment of the 17. SS-Panzergrenadier-Division, reinforced by the battered but experienced paratroopers of Fallschirmjäger-Rgt. 6.

The attack down the Carentan–Périers road stalled almost immediately. The green infantry had no experience in *bocage* fighting and the accompanying tanks were equally unprepared for the dense hedgerows. An attempt to reinvigorate the attack by the two lead regiments in the afternoon seemed to get some traction in one regimental sector, only to have the regiment pushed back by a German counter-attack around dark. The German paratroop commander, Friedrich von der Heydte, returned captured US medical personnel with a note saying that the 83rd Division probably needed them.

Collins pushed Gen. Macon of the 83rd Division to resume his attack on July 5, with the reserve regiment substituted for the bloodied 330th Infantry. The advance on the 5th was as disappointing as the first day, though the forward battalions beat back several German counter-attacks. Collins realized that the division's inexperience was at the heart of the problems but he had few options in such constricted terrain. His other unit, the 4th Infantry Division, was battle hardened but had taken 5,400 casualties in June and its rifle companies were filled with nearly 4,400 new replacements.

A 105mm M3 howitzer of the 4th Division engages targets south of Carentan on July 11. Each infantry regiment had a cannon company with 12 of these howitzers, a smaller and lighter cannon than the more familiar M2A1 105mm howitzer used in field artillery battalions.

Of the 27 rifle company commanders who had landed with the division on Utah Beach on D-Day, all but five had been killed or wounded in the June fighting. The situation with platoon commanders was even worse. In spite of these issues, Collins decided to subordinate the 331st Infantry from the 83rd Division to Barton's 4th Infantry Division headquarters, and to add the experienced 12th Infantry Regiment to the attack.

The third and fourth days of the attack went no better than the previous two days in spite of the additions from the 4th Infantry Division. The regiments of the 83rd Division by this stage were short of about 600 men each, but the division began to show signs of improvement in its performance as its riflemen gained combat experience. The VII Corps attack had fallen far short of its intended goal of Sainteny and had only penetrated about 2½ miles into the German defenses. However, German casualties had also been high and Hausser was obliged to commit the last reserve battalion in this sector to the front on July 7 in the hope of restraining the American advance. The situation around La Haye-du-Puits and Carentan was so serious that on the 7th, Hausser was finally able to convince OB West to permit the transfer of the 5. Fallschirmjäger-Division from Brittany to Normandy.

The VII Corps offensive continued through July 16 at which point actions west of the Taute River were halted in anticipation of Operation *Cobra*. Some actions east of the Taute continued, mainly to secure better jumping-off points for Operation *Cobra*. The fighting in the narrow isthmus from July 9 to 16 gained about 6 square miles of terrain at a cost of 4,800 casualties. Losses were especially high in the tormented 4th Division, which suffered 2,300 casualties including three of nine battalion commanders and nine of 27 rifle company commanders in the early July fighting.

THE XIX CORPS VIRE RIVER BRIDGEHEAD

The third corps to enter the offensive was Corlett's XIX Corps located immediately north of St Lô. Its dispositions reflected the terrain of this sector. It had penetrated further south on its left (eastern) flank since the countryside was generally more open. Its right flank on the east bank of the Vire–Taute Canal was in dense *bocage* country with numerous water obstructions. The corps had two battered but experienced units, the 9th and 29th Divisions, and a new unit, the 30th Division. The 3rd Armored Division was in corps reserve.

The initial attack on Friday, July 7 began in the 30th Division sector facing the 17. SS-Panzergrenadier-Division. The initial attack was intended to push the 30th Division over the Vire River and the Vire–Taute Canal to the west bank. The 30th Division commander, Leland Hobbs, decided to use the 117th Infantry for the initial water crossing near Aire since the regiment had been the river-crossing demonstration unit at the Fort Benning infantry school. The water obstacles were not especially wide but the ground around them had been flooded and did not provide a solid basis for moving heavy bridging equipment. A major engineering effort was planned with both divisional and corps battalions. The assault waves would ford across using assault boats. The engineers would then follow with footbridges, an infantry pontoon bridge, a floating treadway bridge and the hasty repair of the stone bridge at Aire.

NORMANDY BUSH WAR (PP. 52–53)

Although the hedgerow fighting might have appeared to be static positional warfare, it was far more dynamic than it first seemed. German "bush war" tactics used a variant of World War I tactics, relying on a thinly-held forward outpost line followed by a main line of resistance one or more hedgerows further behind. The outpost line was intended to detect an advancing enemy formation and force the enemy troops to ground where they would be vulnerable to mortar and artillery fire. Once the enemy force was pinned down by the machine-gun defenses in the outpost line, small fire teams further back in the defenses would be sent forward to strike the attackers from their flank.

The illustration here shows one of these fire teams of the 3. Fallschirmjäger-Division (1) in action outside St Lô in the middle of July 1944. American hedgerow tactics began to evolve into combined-arms tactics with tanks providing direct fire support for the leading wave of attacking riflemen as a method to overcome the deadly German machine-gun nests. Although many accounts have derided American tactics as clumsy and inept, a German Heeresgruppe B study of Bush War tactics remarked of American tank-infantry combat that "We cannot do better than to adopt the combat tactics of the enemy with all his ruses and tricks."

To deal with the threat of American tanks in the *bocage*, the German teams depended on new anti-tank weapons such as the Panzerschreck and Panzerfaust rocket launchers. The Panzerschreck 88mm rocket launcher (2) began to appear in service in the autumn of 1943, and was well integrated into German infantry tactics by the summer of 1944. This was a large, crew-served weapon that required the support of additional loaders to carry additional rounds of rocket ammunition. These weapons were deployed in a special anti-tank company in each regiment, usually with three platoons which could then be distributed to each of the battalions. The Panzerfaust (3) began appearing in Normandy later that the Panzerschreck, and there were initial difficulties with the weapon due to firing malfunctions. These were disposable, one-shot weapons and so the number available at any one time could vary enormously.

The German Army depended on the squad machine gun, usually an MG 42, as the basis of its infantry tactics. In contrast, the Fallschirmjäger force wished to deepen its firepower though the use of the advanced FG 42 assault rifle (4). In the event, the FG 42 was complicated and expensive to manufacture, and so it was never deployed in sufficient numbers. Most German paratroopers were forced to rely on the 98K rifle, sometimes supplemented by small numbers of FG 42s.

An M4 dozer tank of the 743rd Tank Battalion crosses the old stone bridge over the Vire River at Airel on July 7. The town had been seized by the 117th Infantry, 30th Division, earlier in the morning. The bridge had been hastily repaired by replacing the gap with treadway bridge sections as seen here.

Corlett's headquarters anticipated that the river/canal crossing would be heavily contested judging from the activity in the two corps sectors to the west. Yet the fighting in the VIII and VII Corps sectors had drawn away a great deal of strength from the Vire River sector, particularly in the case of the 17. SS-Panzergrenadier-Division. The main opposition in this sector was Kampfgruppe Heintz, attached to the 17. SS-Panzergrenadier-Division. This battlegroup had four battalions each averaging about 400 combat effectives,

The advance of CCB, 3rd Armored Division over the Vire River near St Fromond on July 9 caused considerable congestion in the restricted road network. Here, a column of M5A1 light tanks from Co. C, 33rd Armored Regiment get caught in a traffic jam with a column of jeeps, half-tracks and M8 armored cars of the 83rd Reconnaissance Battalion on the road between La Vautaire and the Saint-Fromond church.

US UNITS

30th Division
1. 1/117th Infantry
2. 2/117th Infantry
3. 3/117th Infantry
4. 1/119th Infantry
5. 2/119th Infantry
6. 3/119th Infantry
7. 1/120th Infantry
8. 2/120th Infantry
9. 3/120th Infantry
10. 743rd Tank Battalion

3rd Armored Division
11. Combat Command A
    Combat Command B
12. Task Force X
13. Task Force Y

14. 113th Cavalry Group

x x
17 ⊠
BAUM

N

x x
2 ⬭
LAMMERDING

LE MESNIL-VENERON

ST JEAN-DE-[

ST DÉSERT

RAULINE

CAVIGNY

▼ EVENTS

1. The 2/117th Infantry makes a crossing of Vire using assault boats at 0430hrs, June 7.

2. Main German defense in this sector after dawn was around the Pont Saint-Fromond stone bridge by elements of the depleted Angers engineer school. German infantry resistance is weak, but artillery from SS-Art.Rgt. 17 and Art.Rgt. 275 is persistent.

3. The Pont Saint-Fromond is repaired; a floating bridge erected on Vire south of the stone bridge by 247th Engineer Combat Batalion; an infantry support bridge erected north of stone bridge by 503rd Light Pontoon Company.

4. All of the 117th Infantry are across the Vire shortly before noon, and moving south.

5. At 1345hrs, the 120th Infantry begins a contested assault across the Vire–Taute Canal with the 3/120th Infantry west of the highway and 1/120th Infantry to the east.

6. 113th Cavalry Group moves across the canal at the bridge starting at 2030hrs to serve as right flank protection.

7. Combat Command B, 3rd Armored Division begins moving over the bridges around 2230hrs at a rate of 45 vehicles per hour.

8. As CCB deploys southward in the early morning of July 8, it is hit by a small counter-attack by PzKpfw IV tanks of 6./SS-Pz.Rgt. 2 of Kampfgrupp Weidinger supported by infantry of Füs.Btl. 275. The German attack is beaten off.

9. Congestion in the bridgehead slows the deployment of the 119th Infantry.

10. The 113th Cavalry Group and the right wing of the 120th Infantry fight against a *Kampfgruppe* from II./SS-Pz.Gren.Rgt. 38 on the western flank of the bridgehead for much of the day.

11. In the afternoon of July 8, Kampfgruppe Wisliceny attempts to counter-attack out of Le Désert with two Panzergrenadier battalions supported by armor, but is halted by heavy artillery fire and the fire from the 743rd Tank Battalion.

12. Schnelle-Brigade 30 is hastily thrown into the fight on the highway to St Jean-de-Daye with little effect. The SS-Panzer-Pioner-Bataillon is instructed to set up blocking positions on the highway south of the hamlet of Rauline.

13. The last reserve of II Fallschirmjager-Korps, its elite Fallschirm-Aüfklarungs-Abt. 12 reconnaissance battalion, is deployed to block the advance of the 120th Infantry east of Le Désert.

14. The only uncommitted element of Kampfgruppe Heintz, I./GR 984, attempts to attack up along the Vire River towards the St Fromond bridge, but makes little headway.

GERMAN UNITS
17. SS-Panzergrenadier-Division "Gotz von Berlichingen"
A. *Kampfgruppe*, II./SS-Pz.Gren.Rgt. 38

Kampfgruppe Heintz
B. I./Grenadier-Regiment 984
C. II./Grenadier-Regiment 984
D. Füsilier-Bataillon 275
E. Armee-Pionier-Schule des AOK 7

F. *Kampfgruppe*, Schnelle-Brigade 30

G. Fallschirm-Aüfklarungs-Abt. 12

2. SS-Panzer-Division "Das Reich"
H. Kampfgruppe Weidinger (I./ SS-Pz.Gren.Rgt. 3 "Deutschland" + 6. Kompanie, SS-Pz.Rgt. 2)
I. Kampfgruppe Wisliceny (II./SS-Pz.Gren.Rgt. 3 "Deutschland")
J. SS-Panzer-Pioner.Abt. 2 "Das Reich"

HOBBS

VIRE–TAUTE CANAL

VIRE RIVER

PONT SAINT-FROMOND

WATSON

THE VIRE RIVER BRIDGEHEAD,
JULY 7–8, 1944

but the battalion covering the bridge across the Vire near Aire/St Fromond was held by the remnants of the 7. Armee engineer school with barely 200 combat effectives.

On the morning of the attack, July 7, the weather was again gloomy with rain and a thick fog in many areas. Artillery preparation began at 0330hrs but air support was cancelled by the low overcast weather. The riflemen of the 117th Infantry began approaching the riverbank under the cover of the dim early morning light around 0430hrs and the artillery began pounding the opposite bank. The lead companies got across the river against stiff but scattered resistance. Repair of the critical stone bridge at Aire was accelerated by using special Brockway bridge erection trucks to lay treadway over the damaged sections. The entire 117th Infantry was over the Vire River by 1000hrs and three vehicular bridges were erected to provide reinforcements. The 120th Infantry next leap-frogged the Vire–Taute Canal at 1330hrs toward St Jean-de-Daye. By the late afternoon, the 30th Division had six of its nine infantry battalions across the water obstacles. By the early evening, the main problem was traffic congestion when a tank battalion and cavalry group began moving to the west bank.

German resistance to the American attack was ineffective. The engineer battalion near Aire was overwhelmed. The two other battalions along the Vire–Taute Canal lost contact with the Kampfgruppe Heintz command post, located well south of St Jean-de-Daye. Some of Füsilier-Bataillon 275 took part in a counter-attack the following day in the St Fromond area, but there was no coordinated counter-attack on the 7th due to the communications breakdown.

The day's operation had gone so well that Bradley committed the 3rd Armored Division to the attack. Corlett instructed the division to begin to move southward in the hopes of quickly reaching the high ground west of St Lô. Coordination between the 3rd Armored Division and Corlett's headquarters was impeded when Corlett became bed-ridden with a severe kidney infection. Major-General Walton Walker, the commander of the uncommitted XX Corps, was brought in to assist. The 3rd Armored Division commander, Maj. Gen. Watson, had not been warned about a possible commitment of his division since no one had expected the advance over the Vire to progress so quickly. He decided to deploy one combat command, CCB under Brig. Gen. John Bohn, as the first wave of the mission.

The German response on the first day was weak. The fighting on the La Haye-du-Puits/Carentan fronts had depleted Hausser's 7. Armee of any significant reserves to counter the Vire River breakthrough. OB West was also very short of reserves. In the short-term, all that was available was Schnelle-Brigade 30, a bicycle-mobile infantry unit that was clearly not adequate for the task with barely two weak battalions. Some small battle-groups from the 2. SS-Panzer-Division with a few tanks were added to stiffen the counter-attack.

The only mobile theater reserve was the Panzer-Lehr-Division in the Panzergruppe West sector that had been pulled out of the line for refurbishment. Both Rommel at Heeresgruppe B headquarters and Kluge at OB West headquarters reluctantly agreed that this unit was the only plausible savior. However, it would take at least two days to move the division to strike the bridgehead since Allied air power meant it had to travel under the cover of darkness.

An M4A1 tank of the 3rd Battalion, 33rd Armored Regiment, CCB, 3rd Armored Division passes a column of knocked out PzKpfw IV Ausf. H tanks of 6./ II./SS-Panzer-Regiment 2, 2-SS-Panzer-Division "Das Reich" beyond St Fromond on July 9 after having crossed the Vire River near St Fromond. These may be the three tanks ambushed that morning by Sgt. Dean Balderson when his tank popped out of an orchard behind the German column and engaged them from the rear at short range.

Combat Command B, 3rd Armored Division, moved over the Vire River on the night of July 7–8 through a series of very constricted roads and river passages. The division was not very experienced at this point, and was hardly ideal for a bold thrust to St Lô. One of its combat commands had previously become embroiled in a short but costly skirmish near Villiers-Fossard on June 29–30. This experience had made the division nervous and very wary of using the road network since it had found that the Germans tended to set up ambushes at cross-roads and other key points. This costly introduction to *bocage* fighting made the division risk-averse.

The CCB spearhead moved very slowly when it tried to advance cross-country out of the Vire bridgehead. Hobbs complained to corps headquarters about the snail's pace of the advance and so XIX Corps headquarters instructed Hobbs to take command of CCB. The 30th Division felt that it had adequate resources to continue the advance including a supporting tank battalion that was better suited to the terrain than an entire combat command. Corlett did not agree and still wanted CCB to spearhead the attack. As a compromise, Bohn was instructed to push CCB ahead to Hauts-Vents and take Hill 91 on the northwest outskirts of Pont-Hébert by 1700hrs. General Hobbs was growing increasingly anxious because his intelligence officers were warning him of the approach of at least two German counter-attack forces from 2. SS-Panzer-Division and Panzer-Lehr-Division.

One of the little-known Achilles' heels of the German formations in Normandy was their vulnerability to Allied signals intelligence interceptions. The problem was that the divisional Flivo (Fliegerverbindungsoffiziere: air cooperation officer) used a vulnerable Luftwaffe code when communicating by radio with higher commands. This code had been broken by the Allied Ultra decryption team. In contrast, other army communications between divisions and army headquarters tended to be conducted by field telephone or teletypes that were not vulnerable to interception. These Luftwaffe radio transmissions were common during the preparation for offensive actions, since the Panzer division commanders had some hope that the Luftwaffe might stage fighter sweeps in support of major Panzer operations. These sweeps were mainly intended to rid the skies of the pesky US Army light artillery spotter aircraft that increased the precision of American artillery strikes. Inadvertently, the attempts to muster Luftwaffe assistance simply warned the Allies of impending actions, and seldom achieved the intended objective of Luftwaffe support.

The first German counter-attacks took place on July 8 but were disjointed and ineffective. Kampfgruppe Wisliceny arrived on the scene with a Panzergrenadier battalion from Pz.Gren.Rgt. 3 "Deutschland." SS-Sturmbannführer Günther Wisliceny took over command of the remains of Kampfgruppe Heintz along with other elements of 2. SS-Panzer-Division in the area. An early morning attack near St Fromond by a company of tanks from SS-Panzer-Rgt. 2 supported by infantry of Kampfgruppe Heintz was quickly smothered. Wisliceny attempted to create a coordinated counter-attack later in the day with a battalion from the 17. SS-Panzergrenadier-Division attacking the Vire–Taute Canal sector to the north west, his own battle group pushing up out of Le Désert from the southwest, the newly arrived Schnelle-Brigade 30 pushing up the main road to St Jean-de-Daye, and a battalion from Kampfgruppe Heintz pushing up the eastern side of the bridgehead along the Vire River. The Allied Ultra decryption team learned of this plan the night before the attack and it was stopped without significant consequence. The attacks continued the following day, but the US units were supported by no fewer than 18 artillery battalions under XIX Corps control which smothered most of the counter-attacks.

While this was taking place, the hapless CCB, 3rd Armored Division, was continuing its mission in a confused and lethargic fashion. One task force made a wrong turn on the road between St Jean-de-Daye and St Lô and lost two tanks when they stumbled into an ambush of 3in. anti-tank guns of the 823rd Tank Destroyer Battalion. The American gun crews had set up a road-block and were assured that no US tanks were operating in their sector.

By nightfall on July 9, a paltry six tanks from CCB 3rd Armored Division finally arrived at Hauts-Vents. After 48 hours of frustration, Hobbs relieved Bohn of command; his place was taken by Col. Dorrance Roysdon. When CCB finally did secure Hill 91 with additional forces on July 11, Hobbs admitted that his relief of Bohn had been premature. The problem had not been Bohn's actions, but rather the decision to commit CCB into a bridgehead much too congested for it to properly deploy. Furthermore, its pre-disposition to avoid using the main roads due to the past experiences at Villiers-Fossard contributed to the loss of an opportunity to seize St Lô in a bold stroke. In the meantime, the 9th Infantry Division had been added to the forces on the west bank of the Vire.

PANZER-LEHR-DIVISION COUNTER-ATTACK AGAINST THE VIRE BRIDGEHEAD

Rommel had warned GFM Günther von Kluge that "if the Vire bridgehead cannot be cleaned out, the whole [7. Armee] front will collapse." In the event that the US Army kept pushing southward, 84. Korps could be cut off from the rest of the Wehrmacht in Normandy with dire consequences. An attack

These two Panther Ausf. A tanks of 1./Panzer-Regiment.6 were knocked out near Le Désert during the failed 11 July attack while supporting Bataillon-Philips of Panzergrenadier-Lehr Rgt. 901. Most of the ten tanks lost during this attack were ambushed by M10 3in. GMC of the 899th Tank Destroyer Battalion. The poor performance of the Panther tank during this attack led the Panzer-Lehr-Division commander, Fritz Bayerlein, to complain that they were not well suited to operations in the *bocage* since their long barrels made it difficult to traverse the turret in the narrow country roads.

using the Panzer-Lehr-Division was slated for July 9, but moving the division into place in such a short time proved impossible. Had the counter-attack been conducted on the 9th as originally planned it might have overcome the modest American forces then in the bridgehead. By July 11, the bridgehead had been substantially reinforced with two entire infantry divisions plus large portions of the 3rd Armored Division. Under such changed circumstances, the attack had become a foolhardy act of desperation. The offensive was conducted without any serious reconnaissance and was based on a serious underestimation of US forces. There was the presumption that a shocking blow in a sector that had never seen a significant Panzer force would be enough to overwhelm the American defenses. However, by this stage of the campaign, both the 9th and 30th Divisions were combat experienced and far more familiar with the conditions of *bocage* fighting than the Panzer-Lehr-Division. Furthermore, the German attack was badly planned with four battalions operating along separate axes in constricted terrain with no ability to support one another.

The Panzer-Lehr-Division had already suffered very heavy attrition in the British/Canadian sector during the June 1944 combat, losing 3,407 men, 50 tanks, 82 half-tracks and over 200 trucks and other vehicles in less than three weeks of fighting. While the 3,407 casualties were only 23 percent of overall strength, it was 48 percent of combat strength. The Panzergrenadier regiments were especially hard hit, falling to only about a third of their authorized combat strength. At this point in time, the replacement system was still functioning and the division received 1,633 replacement troops. The division also received 19 replacement tanks by early July.

Allied intelligence was tracking the progress of the Panzer-Lehr-Division's transfer from the British to American sectors, and had a reasonably sound idea about the intended German attack. It is not clear how much detail from the Ultra decrypts reached tactical commanders. Most of the official histories covering this period were written before the declassification of the "Ultra Secret" and even wartime records do not directly mention Ultra intelligence.

However, it would appear that corps and divisional headquarters received some detail, even if the source of the information was never specified.

The Panzer-Lehr-Division attack was conducted by two battle-groups based on the two Panzergrenadier regiments, each consisting of roughly two Panzergrenadier battalions, a company of Pioner and one or more companies of tanks. Kampfgruppe 901 launched its attack on the left flank from the area south of the Bois du Hommet, aimed at St Jean-de-Daye and the Vire–Taute Canal crossing site. Kampfgruppe 902 was on the right flank and pushed out of the towns of Hauts-Vents and Pont-Hébert with the ultimate objective being to clear out the St Fromond/Aire bridgehead. The terrain did not favor the use of armored half-tracks, so the Panzergrenadiers mounted up on the tanks and assault guns.

The attack began in the pre-dawn hours of July 11. Bataillon-Philips (I./Pz.Gren.Rgt. 901) riding on Panther tanks made the deepest penetration of the day, crashing into the 39th Infantry, 9th Division, near the village of Le Désert. However, two companies of M10 3in. GMC of the 899th Tank Destroyer Battalion were supporting the infantry regiment. Knowing the terrain far better than the German tank crews, they maneuvered their tank destroyers and began engaging the Panthers in the dark. When the first Panther was hit and exploded, the resulting fire illuminated the column, making it vulnerable to attack by the other tank destroyers. Bataillon-Philips, numbering 250 men and ten Panther tanks, was surrounded and wiped out; only 30 men escaped.

Kampfgruppe 902 on the right flank penetrated about a mile but was less successful in disrupting the 30th Division positions. One of its two attack groups, II./Pz.Gren.Rgt. 902, ran headlong into Task Force Y of CCB 3rd Armored Division and was immediately stopped. Although there was considerable chaos in the American positions before daybreak, the US units quickly rallied. As the US Army had learned in the previous weeks of fighting, the *bocage* terrain favored the defender over the attacker. By noon, it was

GIs of the 9th Division gawk at a burned-out Panther Ausf. A of 1./Panzer-Regiment 6 that was hit by fire from an M10 3in. GMC of the 899th Tank Destroyer Battalion during the failed attack near Le Désert.

A well emplaced 75mm PaK 40 anti-tank gun of the 3. Fallschirmjager-Division camouflaged in a hedgerow near St Lô. FJR 5 and FJR 9 had two of these in their 14. Kompanie. They were usually deployed to cover key roads.

evident that the attack had failed. The Panzer-Lehr attack did little more than delay the advance of the 9th Infantry Division by a day, but cost Panzer-Lehr-Division about 500–700 casualties, ten Panther and eight PzKpfw IV tanks.

Following the failed attack, the Panzer-Lehr-Division was given a sector of the front to defend, roughly 5km wide. The defense was based on two *Kampfgruppen* organized around the Panzergrenadier regiments with Kampfgruppe Welsch (Pz.Gren.Rgt. 902) holding the right sector and Kampfgruppe Scholze (Pz.Gren.Rgt. 901) holding the left sector. The defenses used typical German tactics with a thinly manned outpost line along the forward edge of battle followed by a string of strongpoints, and then the mobile reserves for counter-attacking. This type of defensive arrangement was a waste of one of the Wehrmacht's best-equipped Panzer divisions. This was the only division in Normandy to have all four Panzergrenadier battalions equipped with armored half-tracks. The half-tracks were useless in the *bocage* country, and so were parked behind the lines about 40km away from the main-line-of-resistance. To make matters worse, a Panzer division had far fewer rifleman than an ordinary infantry division and both Panzergrenadier regiments had been decimated in the previous fighting. Their usual advantage on the battlefield was their mobility and the extra firepower available on their half-tracks, but these advantages were thrown away when deployed in a static defense line. While it was not clear at the time, the weakness of the Panzer-Lehr-Division defense line was the critical ingredient in the eventual success of the Operation *Cobra* break-through later in July.

EAST OF THE VIRE

While 30th Division was engaged with the Panzer-Lehr-Division in the Vire bridgehead, the rest of XIX Corps to the east of the Vire River was assigned to press southward towards St Lô. The newly arrived 35th Division was

GERMAN UNITS

Panzer-Lehr-Division

Kampfgruppe 901
A. Bataillon-Philips (I./Pz.Gren.Rgt. 901 + 1./ Pz.Rgt. 6)
B. Bataillon-Schöne (II./Pz.Gren.Rgt. 901 + 2./Pz.Rgt. 6)
Kampfgruppe 902
C. Bataillon-Kuhnow (I./Pz.Gren.Rgt. 902 + 8./Pz.Rgt. Lehr)
D. Bataillon-Böhm (II./Pz.Gren.Rgt. 902 + 7./Pz.Rgt. Lehr)

2. SS-Panzer-Division "Das Reich"
E. Kampfgruppe Wisliceny

275. Infanterie-Division
F. Kampfgruppe Heintz

ST JEAN-DE-D.

LE MESNIL-VENERON

LA CAPLAINERIE

LA CHARLEMAGNERIE

LE

GRAIGNÉE

LE MESNIL-ANGOT

9 | EDDY

PANZER-LEHR | BAYERLEIN

2 | LAMMERDING

▼ EVENTS

1. In the pre-dawn hours around 0330hrs, July 11, Bataillon-Schöne moves up a gap between the 47th Infantry and the 39th Infantry along the contemporary D445 road. Around 0530hrs, trailing Panzergrenadier troops overran the command post of the 3/47th Infantry.

2. Bataillon-Philips pushes up the D8 road into the village of Le Désert starting around 0330hrs, splitting the two battalions of the 39th Infantry on either side of the road. The column attempts to overrun the command post of 2/39th Infantry on the north side of the village, but is repulsed by 57mm gun and bazooka fire in a series of skirmishes lasting over two hours.

3. The 3/39th Infantry, the regiment's reserve, is instructed to move forward and block the D8 road from Le Desert to St Jean-de-Daye. This forces the spearhead of Bataillon-Philips further northward on the D445 road towards the hamlets of La Caplainerie and La Charlemagnerie.

4. The 1/47 Infantry, the regimental reserve, is ordered forward out of La Charlemagnerie down the D445 road to block Bataillon-Philips along this axis. They are supported by four M10 3in. GMC of Co. C, 899th Tank Destroyer Battalion.

5. Company A, 899th Tank Destroyer Battalion stationed east of Le Désert, engages the southern spearhead of Bataillon-Philips about 500 yards outside the town. One Panther tank and one M10 tank destroyer are knocked out, and the two other Panther tanks withdraw.

6. After dawn, a column of Panther tanks approaches La Charlemagnerie. The lead tank is knocked out by an M10 tank destroyer of C/899th Tank Destroyer Battalion. To the east, the Panthers engage in a duel with two M10 tank destroyers. One M10 damages a Panther before being knocked out, but the other tank destroyer knocks out the damaged Panther and then burns out a second with flank shots. The M10 tank destroyers accompanying the 1/47th Infantry engage and destroy three Panther tanks.

7. At 0900hrs, three sorties of P-51 and P-47 fighters were directed again Kampfgruppe 901 troops and vehicles in Le Hommet d'Arthenay and claim to have knocked out 13 of 14 tanks.

8. By 1600hrs, Bataillon-Philips has been surrounded and destroyed by elements of the 39th and 47th Infantry and Bataillon-Schöne has retreated back to its start line.

9. The initial attack of Bataillon-Böhm from Kampfgruppe 902 ran directly into the defenses of 3/120th Infantry, penetrating as far as the battalion command post in the pre-dawn darkness. The attack is hit hard by machine-gun and bazooka fire and fails to make a penetration of the American defenses. By the time the fighting ends around mid-morning, Bataillon-Böhm had lost five PzKpfw IV tanks, four SdKfz 251 half-tracks and about 60 prisoners.

10. Bataillon-Kuhnow with seven PzKpfw IV tanks launched its attack out of Pont-Hébert pushing up the D446 road along the Vire River where 3/119th Infantry had few defenses. At least one tank reached about 1 mile behind US lines and was sited near La Cocquerie.

11. Other elements of the 119th Infantry that had been preparing to support a Task-Force Y, 3rd Armored Division attack later that day were instead directed to clean up the Bataillon-Kuhnow penetration. They knocked out two PzKpfw IV tanks with the support of the 823rd Tank Destroyer Battalion near Bahais.

12. Task Force Y spends the day cleaning up other scattered elements of Bataillon-Kuhnow that had infiltrated along the Vire River.

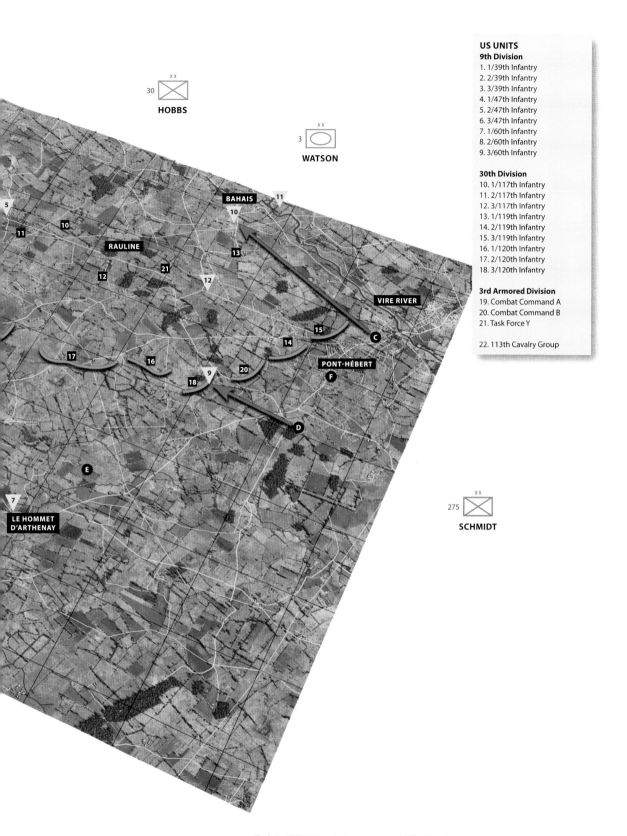

PANZER-LEHR ATTACK, JULY 11, 1944

US UNITS

9th Division
1. 1/39th Infantry
2. 2/39th Infantry
3. 3/39th Infantry
4. 1/47th Infantry
5. 2/47th Infantry
6. 3/47th Infantry
7. 1/60th Infantry
8. 2/60th Infantry
9. 3/60th Infantry

30th Division
10. 1/117th Infantry
11. 2/117th Infantry
12. 3/117th Infantry
13. 1/119th Infantry
14. 2/119th Infantry
15. 3/119th Infantry
16. 1/120th Infantry
17. 2/120th Infantry
18. 3/120th Infantry

3rd Armored Division
19. Combat Command A
20. Combat Command B
21. Task Force Y

22. 113th Cavalry Group

HOBBS 30

WATSON 3

BAHAIS

RAULINE

VIRE RIVER

PONT-HÉBERT

LE HOMMET D'ARTHENAY

SCHMIDT 275

assigned to push down the eastern side of the Vire River in concert with the 30th Division on the western side. Further to the east around Villiers-Fossard, the 29th Division was poised to strike towards the Martinville Ridge. The 2nd Infantry Division of the neighboring V Corps was assigned to push down to the St Lô highway after seizing Hill 192. The terrain in this sector was dense *bocage*, and the objectives were mainly the hills and ridgelines that paralleled the St Lô–Bayeux highway.

Two of the units in this attack, the 2nd and 29th Divisions, had been involved in *bocage* fighting since mid-June and were well aware of its many pitfalls. Both divisions were convinced that better tank-infantry cooperation was essential to tactical success. These units were aware that the *bocage* could be penetrated using tank dozers. However, the supporting tank battalions seldom had their nominal complement of four dozers, and these often became combat casualties or suffered from breakdowns after repeated attempts to punch through the dense hedgerows. Some other more plentiful alternative was needed. Both divisions were experimenting with different tactical innovations.

The 2nd Infantry Division came up with the idea of preparing *bocage* along the start line for tank penetration. The troops would surreptitiously hollow out openings in the hedgerows, leaving enough soil and shrubbery facing the German lines to conceal the openings. At the start of the attack, the supporting tanks would charge across the fields and burst through the openings, enabling the lead assault teams to reach the next hedgerow before the Germans could bring up anti-tank weapons. From past experience, the division expected that the German defense line would be shallow and only two or three hedgerows deep in most sectors. To deal with the subsequent hedgerows, the tanks were supplied by engineer demolition charges to rapidly breach the hedgerows. The most effective technique developed for the attack was the preparation of extremely detailed 1:10,000 scale maps

A .30-cal. light machine gun squad deployed in the edge of a hedgerow during the fighting near Hill 192 on July 11. The assistant gunner is armed with a .45-cal. M3 "grease gun" instead of the usual .30-cal. carbine.

of the *bocage* in front of each regiment. These were provided to the infantry, tank, and artillery units and had prepared codenames to facilitate artillery targeting. The tank tactics developed by the 29th Division were somewhat more elaborate and are described in more detail in the accompanying Battlescene here.

Besides the "salad fork" hedgerow cutters employed by the 29th Division, there are records that indicate that other tank units in the neighboring V Corps fielded "brush cutters" on their tanks in July; however, details are lacking. These were a type of plow using a length of railroad rail fixed to the front of the tank. These devices were evolutionary antecedents of the better-known Culin "Rhinoceros" hedgerow cutter that saw its combat debut during Operation *Cobra* later in July 1944.

Another innovation first developed at this time was the addition of a standard EE-8 field telephone on the back of the tanks. The field telephone was wired into the tank's intercom system, and the field telephone fitted in a .30-cal. ammo box at the rear of the tank. An accompanying rifleman or engineers could thereby immediately communicate with the tank crew instead of relying on the elaborate protocol needed if trying to interface the incompatible infantry and tank radios.

Prior to the final push on St Lô, the 29th Division commander, Maj. Gen. Charles Gebhardt, created a special training course near Couvains to instruct his troops on new tactics and techniques for hedgerow fighting. He is seen here on July 18 with one of his staff officers, Maj. William Bratton.

The 29th Division commander, Maj. Gen. Charles Gebhardt, ordered the creation of a special training area near Couvains prior to a planned assault. The M4 medium tanks and infantry squads practised a variety of new tactics to fight in the hedgerows, including the new explosive breaching technique. Another tactical change was to convince the riflemen to cross the hedgerow square through the center, not along the lateral hedgerows on the sides of the fields. The sides offered the false promise of shelter, but the German practice was to position a machine gun in each corner that could mow down any infantry squad moving along the side hedgerow. These combined arms tactics were summarized as "One squad, one tank, one field."

THE MARTINVILLE RIDGE

The center of the XIX Corps attack was the 29th Division, fighting on the northeast approaches of St Lô. The attack was conducted primarily by the 115th and 116th Infantry Regiments. The 116th Infantry faced the defenses of II./FS-Rgt. 9, holding positions on the Martinville Ridge, also known as Hill 147. The attack started with methodical tank-infantry attacks. The German

BUSTING THE *BOCAGE* (PP. 68–69)

By mid-July 1944, several units in the First US Army were developing new techniques to permit tanks to cut through the hedgerow. While this could be accomplished using dozer tanks, at most there were four of these tanks per battalion. The 747th Tank Battalion **(1)**, attached to the 29th Division, worked with Lt. Col. Robert Ploger's 121st Engineer Combat Battalion to develop ways to rapidly breach the *bocage*. During an attack on June 24, 1944, the engineers placed a pair of 24-pound charges 8ft apart at the base of a hedge. This did blow a gap large enough for a tank to pass through, but the engineers decided that a charge double the size was really needed. Ploger began a more careful study of the problem. A tank company, penetrating 1½ miles through *bocage* country, would on average encounter 34 separate hedgerows. This would require 17 tons of explosive per company or about 60 tons per battalion. This was clearly beyond the resources of any engineer battalion. Ploger and the tankers continued to experiment with explosive breaching, and found that a much smaller charge could be used if it could be buried deep within

the base of the hedge. However, digging holes in the hedge while under fire was both time-consuming and dangerous. One of the tankers came up with the idea of fitting a pair of timber prongs on the front of each tank, called a "salad fork" **(2)**. When a breach in the *bocage* was needed, a tank would charge across the field and embed the prongs in the base of the hedge. When the tank backed out, it would pull out the timber prong, leaving small tunnels **(3)**. The engineers pre-packaged 15 pounds of explosive in the fiber-board containers used to transport 105mm artillery ammunition **(4)**. Two of these improvised demolition charges could create a gap wide enough for a tank and the accompanying infantry. Small M29 Weasel tracked utility vehicles would follow the tank-engineer team, bringing along extra explosives, as seen here **(5)**. The use of these tactics in combat in mid-July had very mixed results with some units feeling that they were too elaborate and time consuming. Neighboring units took the salad fork idea one step further and developed the "Rhino" hedge-cutter that permitted a tank to breach a hedgerow without the need for explosives.

The attack on the Martinville Ridge on July 15–16 by the 29th Division was supported by specially modified tanks of the 747th Tank Battalion, fitted with two timber prongs on the bow to create cavities in the base of hedgerows. After impaling the timber prongs into the hedgerow, the tank withdrew and accompanying engineers filled the cavities with prepared explosive charges to blow gaps into the hedgerows.

outpost line was especially well defended as well as being heavily mined. After a slow start, the 116th Infantry attack began to pick up momentum, and the 2/116th Infantry began to reach its objective to the east of Martinville by afternoon. The pace of the advance was good enough that by mid-afternoon, Gen. Gebhardt encouraged the 116th Infantry to try to reach St Lô itself. Even after the 175th Infantry was sent to reinforce the advance, the objective was beyond its grasp. The advance of the 116th Infantry was assisted by the fighting in the neighboring 2nd Infantry Division sector, especially the success of the 23rd Infantry around Hill 192 as described below.

In contrast to the steady progress by the 116th Infantry, the neighboring 115th Infantry had a very hard time and was unable to take its objectives, the small villages of La Luzerne and Belle-Fontaine. In spite of the lack of progress, German casualties continued to mount, in no small measure due to the heavy American divisional artillery support that totaled 13,000 rounds that day alone.

A paratrooper armed with one of the rare FG 42 automatic rifles with its distinctive side magazine. These were built in very small numbers, around 7,000, and it probably identifies him as serving in one of the *Sturmtruppen* of Fallschirm-Aufklarungs-Abteilung 12, the corps-level reconnaissance battalion of II Fallschirmjäger-Korps that was equipped with this weapon.

HILL 192

For the 2nd Infantry Division, no objective had greater symbolic importance that Hill 192. This small hill was located to the east of the village of St André de l'Épine. Since the farmland to the immediate north was largely flat, the hill provided vistas to the Vire River and Caumont, allowing the Germans to observe all US movements towards St. Lô in this area. The 2nd Division had attempted to capture this hill nearly a month earlier on June 16, losing 1,250 men in the process without gaining control of the hill. During the lull in fighting in this sector in late June and early July, the 3. Fallschirmjäger-Division had continued to reinforce their strongpoints. Even though there were few infantry clashes during this period, both sides exchanged mortar and artillery fire on a daily basis, and the 3. Fallschirmjäger -Division reported suffering a hundred casualties per day to the incessant bombardment.

The 2nd Division attack on Hill 192 was conducted by two of its three regiments, the 23rd and 38th Infantry, with the 9th Infantry remaining in division reserve. Only two battalions of the 23rd Infantry and one from the 38th Infantry were directly involved in the attack. Hill 192 itself was held by two German paratrooper battalions, III./ Fallschirmjager-Rgt. 9 near the crest of the hill facing the 38th Infantry, and I./Fallschirmjager.Rgt. 5 on the eastern side of the hill facing the 23rd Infantry. By this time, the German paratroopers had a well-established, multi-layered defensive position with each field covered by one or more machine guns, and every hedge line and road pre-registered by regimental mortar crews. As a result, the force ratio was about 3:2 in favor of the attacking American force, by no means an overwhelming advantage in terrain that favored the defender. The main American advantage remained the heavy artillery support, with some 20,000 rounds being fired in support of the July 11 attack.

V Corps had planned to conduct air strikes at the start of the attack, but ground haze prevented the planned air support. The attack was preceded by a major artillery attack, including a heavy mix of white phosphorous (WP) rounds, nominally a smoke round but with a significant incendiary effect. "Willy Pete" was much feared and hated by the German troops. The WP

A defensive position of the 3. Fallschirmjäger-Division carved into a hedgerow outside St Lô with a dead GI in the foreground.

This Panther Ausf. A tank number 232 of 2. Kompanie, Panzer-Lehr-Regiment 130 was captured during the fighting near the Vire River north of St Lô. It was put back into service by the 29th Division for trials as seen here near Balleroy on July 16, 1944.

projectiles fragmented into small shards of incandescent white phosphorus that caused excruciating burns in contact with flesh; the smoke was irritating and could be toxic in sufficient concentration.

Companies E and F, 2/38th Infantry, made a methodical advance towards the west side of Hill 192, encountering especially tough resistance in the hamlet of Cloville. This was one of the few sectors with German armored support, apparently two StuG III from FS.StuG.Brigade 12. The fixed casemates on these assault guns made them very clumsy in the *bocage*, and both were knocked in duels with accompanying US tanks of the 741st Tank Battalion. The two rifle companies eventually cleared the Le Soulaire Farm and made it over the west side of Hill 192 to reach the objective of the St Lô–Bayeux highway.

The neighboring 1/38th Infantry, advancing towards the center of Hill 192, was hit such intense fire that the six accompanying M4 tanks of A/741st Tank Battalion were knocked out or forced to withdraw. Two of its companies managed to fight their way up Hill 192 by methodically overcoming the German paratrooper defenses in each of the hedgerows. The 1/38th Infantry reached the reverse slope of Hill 192 by early afternoon, but was only able to advance to within about 200 yards of its objective along the St Lô–Bayeux highway.

The 1/23rd Infantry faced the unenviable task of pushing over a ravine, already notorious in the division as "Purple Heart Draw." The ravine was steep enough that it could not be negotiated by tanks and the task of breaching the draw was assigned to the 1st Platoon, Co. A, 23rd Infantry. The platoon came under intense machine-gun and mortar fire, even though four M4 tanks of A/741st Tank Battalion attempted to offer covering fire from the edge of the ravine. About two-thirds of the platoon became casualties in the ensuing fighting. Eventually, two other platoons from Co. A, supported by two M4 tanks of C/741st Tank Battalion, were able to maneuver to the opposite side of the gully and reduce the stubborn German strongpoint covering it. The 1/23rd Infantry eventually advanced to within 400 yards of its objective, the St Lô–Bayeux highway.

Mortars were one of the most effective weapons in the *bocage* fighting since the mortar bombs could be dropped over a hedgerow with considerable precision. This is an 81mm mortar of the 35th Division in action along the Vire River on July 14. Each rifle battalion had six of these in their weapons company.

While the main attack was underway, Co. L of 3/23rd Infantry reduced a major German strongpoint in the *bocage* near St Georges d'Elle. This also served to tie down other elements of the 3. Fallschirmjäger-Division and prevent them from reinforcing the embattled defenders around Hill 192.

Although only one American company managed to reach the St Lô–Bayeux highway by the end of the day, the attack had been successful in overcoming the German defenses on Hill 192. German casualties had been high, including 147 prisoners. The 3. Fallschirmjäger-Division was forced to commit its last reserve, the engineers of FS-Pioner.Kompanie 3. Due to heavy losses, the German counter-attack launched late on July 11 was too feeble to push back the American line. The extent of German losses was evident in the fighting on the 12th. III./FS-Rgt. 9 had suffered a further 600 casualties, completely reducing its combat effectiveness. It was replaced by III./FS-Rgt. 8 and its troops attempted to erect a new defense line south of the St Lô–Bayeux highway. The 2nd Infantry Division secured the St Lô–Bayeux highway as far as La Calvarie. Two days of fighting cost the 2nd Infantry Division 69 dead, 328 wounded and 8 missing.

The attack by the 2nd Infantry Division assisted the progress of the neighboring 29th Division. As on July 11–12, the 29th Division attack on Thursday, July 13 was conducted primarily by the 115th and 116th Infantry Regiments. The 116th Infantry was able to push over the St Lô–Bayeux highway, and Gen. Gebhardt attempted to reinforce this advance by using his reserve, the 175th Infantry. Due to the congestion in the narrow attack sector, this did not increase the momentum of the attack. After nightfall, the 175th Infantry relieved the battered 116th Infantry on the St. Lô road. There was little infantry fighting on Friday, July 14 since there were incessant summer downpours that turned the battlefield into a sea of mud. Both sides used the lull to regroup. In the three days of intense fighting, the 3. Fallschirmjäger-Division had suffered a staggering 4,064 casualties, and FS-Rgt. 9 was no longer combat effective.

NORTH OF ST LÔ

The third unit to take part in the Tuesday, July 11 offensive was the new and inexperienced 35th Division. This division arrived to the northwest of the 29th Division on the night of July 9/10 with little time to familiarize itself with the terrain. More importantly, the division had no experience at all in *bocage* fighting, nor any specialized training. One of its regiments was in corps reserve so the attack was conducted by only two regiments, the 137th Infantry on the left and 320th Infantry on the right. It was facing the battered but experienced 352. Infanterie-Division and its assortment of battle-groups. Grenadier-Regiment 987 held the critical sector on the east side of the Vire River while GR 916 held the main approach route to St Lô.

MSgt. Efrain Ackerman, a US Army intelligence translator, interviews Oberleutnant Kurt Lingsleben of Schnelle-Brigade 30. This unit had been formed in Normandy in February 1944 from mountain troops, and Lingsleben still has the Edelweiss insignia of the Gebirgsjäger on his field cap. Schnelle-Brigade 30 was one of several units amalgamated to the 352. Infanterie-Division outside St Lô in the hopes of keeping it combat-effective.

The division's attack on July 11 made some gains in the western sector of the 137th Infantry against GR 987, but little on the right against GR 916. Very little progress was made towards its objective, the northern side of the Vire River northwest of St Lô. As in the case of other inexperienced divisions in Normandy, it took time for the division to become acquainted with the unique challenges of *bocage* fighting. By July 14, the 137th Infantry had pushed forward along the Vire River, bringing it even with the 30th Infantry Division on the western side of the Vire. The 137th Infantry faced

Allied air-strikes substantially undermined German logistics in Normandy. This is a column of Skoda Diesel 706 heavy trucks that were hit along the road north of St Lô during the second week of July 1944.

a particularly formidable strongpoint around the hamlet of Le Carrillon. The 352. Infanterie-Division suffered 986 casualties in two days of fighting and committed its last paltry reserves when its main-line-of-resistance was penetrated.

THE ORIGINS OF OPERATION *COBRA*

Even though the *bocage* fighting during the first week of July had been painfully slow, Bradley began to appreciate from intelligence briefings that Hausser's 7. Armee was exhausting the very last of its reserves. There was little evidence of any effort to create a second defensive line deeper in France. Around July 8, Bradley began to formulate a plan to penetrate the German main-line-of-resistance using a carpet-bombing attack, after which he would push through his two heavy armored divisions for the break-out and exploitation. His immediate objective was to push far enough south to permit VIII Corps to swing westward into Brittany, a major operational goal of the *Overlord* plans for the Allied forces in Normandy. After going over details of the plan with the staff of the FUSA headquarters, Bradley presented

Prelude to *Cobra*, July 14–20, 1944

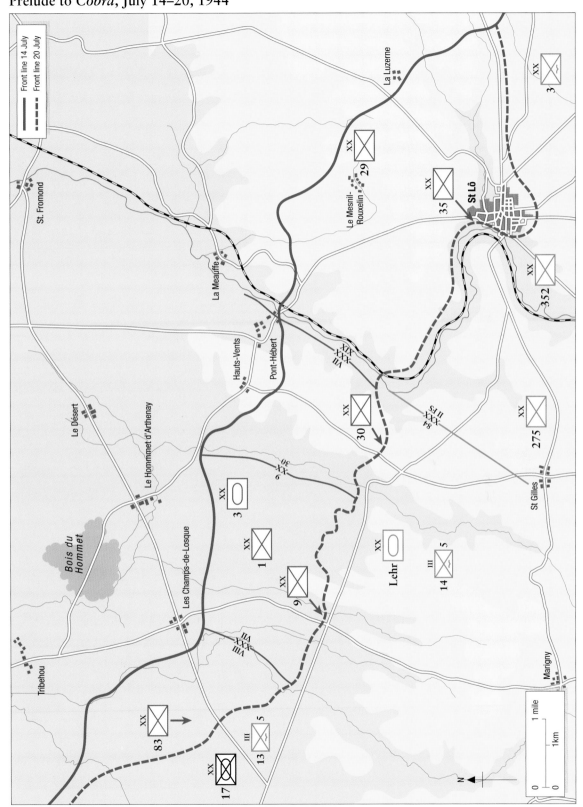

Front line 14 July
Front line 20 July

La Luzerne

St. Fromond

Le Mesnil-Rouxelin

La Meauffe

Hauts-Vents

Pont-Hébert

Le Désert

Le Hommet d'Arthenay

Bois du Hommet

Les Champs-de-Losque

Tribehou

St Lô

St Gilles

Marigny

N

1 mile
1km

the plan to Montgomery on July 10. Montgomery approved the plan, but recommended reinforcing the sector in the main attack zone. The focal point was expected to be in Collin's VII Corps sector, and Collins recommended a section of the Periers–St Lô road as the jumping-off point. After winning Eisenhower's approval, Bradley detailed the Operation *Cobra* plan to the corps commanders and senior staff at his headquarters on July 12. The original plan called for a start of the operation on the 18th, but as will be related below, the start date had to be pushed back several times for a variety of reasons.

The decision to proceed with Operation *Cobra* shaped FUSA plans for the fighting in the third week of July around St Lô. In the VII Corps sector, the 9th and 30th Infantry Divisions needed to gain better start points by reaching the Periers–St Lô road. In the XIX Corps sector, St Lô had to be finally taken since it was a major road junction that would eventually be needed once the *Cobra* breakthrough had been attained.

THE FINAL ASSAULT ON ST LÔ

A .30-cal. light machine gun firing position cut into a hedgerow during the fighting on July 15. The weapons platoon in each rifle company had two light machine-gun squads, each with one of these weapons.

The final attacks towards St Lô started on Saturday, July 15. Although the American focus was mainly in XIX Corps with the largely symbolic mission of capturing St Lô, the focus by Hausser's 7. Armee was on the fighting west of the Vire. An American penetration in this area continued to threaten to cut off Choltitz's 84. AK from the rest of the Wehrmacht in Normandy. The profound weakness of 7. Armee after two weeks of savage "bush war" finally had led to the consent from Berlin to transfer two more units from Brittany into Normandy. The first to arrive was the 5. Fallschirmjäger-Division. While this might seem to be a major addition to the defenses in view of the sterling performance of 3. Fallschirmjäger-Division, OB West had been reluctant to move the 5. Fallschirmjäger-Division into Normandy due to its incomplete training. Most alarming was the shortage of trained officers. The commander of FS-Rgt. 6, Oberst Friedrich von der Heydte, offered a scathing assessment of its shortcomings: "The 5. Fallschirmjäger-Division was of little combat value. Less than 10% of the men had jump training, and barely 20% of the officers had infantry training or experience. Armament and equipment was incomplete; only 50% of the authorized machine guns, one regiment without helmets, no heavy anti-tank weapons, no motorization."

This assessment proved correct and the initial commitment of the unit was disappointing "confirming our experience

The Capture of St Lô

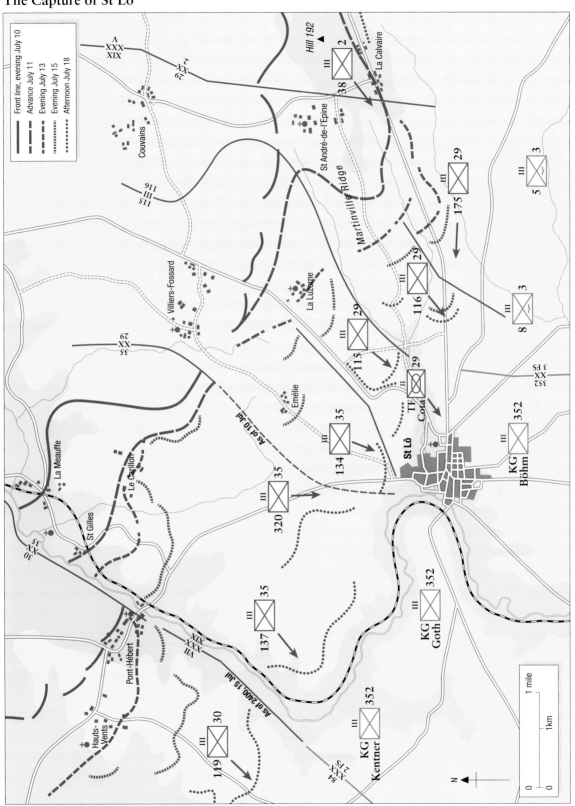

Front line, evening July 10
Advance July 11
Evening July 13
Evening July 15
Afternoon July 18

A VW Schwimmwagen amphibious car of the 3. Fallschirmjager-Division was ambushed by a US tank in a narrow road between the hedgerows outside St Lô on July 15 and its crew killed by machine-gun fire.

that newly committed troops which have not developed teamwork and are thrown into intense combat without having been broken in, suffer disproportionately heavy losses" according to a 7. Armee report. As a result, the division was not deployed intact, but its regiments detached to reinforce other divisions. Fallschirmjäger-Regiment 14 was subordinated to the Panzer-Lehr-Division. Its three battalions were rated at strong, average, and weak, and the divisional commander, Fritz Bayerlein, complained that they were "almost useless as nearly all the time they avoided contact" and discipline was so poor that "in the rear area, there were paratroopers rambling everywhere." Following the 5. Fallschirmjäger-Division was the rest of the 275. Infanterie-Division from Brittany which had already provided one of its regiments as Kampfgruppe Heintz earlier in the campaign. It was slated to become the 7. Armee reserve once it arrived.

The American attacks west of the Vire were conducted by the 30th Division, facing a mixed defense by the Panzer-Lehr-Division consisting of its battered Pz.Gren.Rgt. 902 and elements of the newly arrived FS.Rgt. 14 of the 5. Fallschirmjäger-Division, supported by dug-in tanks. The first day's attack on July 15 secured unimpressive gains, but on the 16th the 120th Infantry finally broke through the main-line-of-resistance along the road from Haut-Vents and pushed through the village of Le Mesnil-Durand. The Panzer-Lehr-Division responded in the afternoon with two vigorous counter-attacks supported by tanks, but these were stymied by heavy US artillery fire. The Panzer-Lehr-Division lost 16 tanks during the day's fighting. The advance by the 30th Division also exposed the west flank of the neighboring 352. Infanterie-Division on the eastern side of the Vire River. Hausser was concerned that it could force its withdrawal back towards St Lô and, as a result, he ordered the Panzer-Lehr-Division to stage another counter-attack against the 30th Division. In view of its weakness in infantry, the German attacks on Monday, July 17 were ineffective though they did slow the American advance.

A rifleman in a foxhole on Rue de Perth on the north side of St Lô opposite the gates of the Château des Commines. The chateau was used as the headquarters for the 84. AK and a large bunker still located in the grounds served as the command post for the corps commander, Gen. Erich Marcks, and Gen. Choltitz after Marcks' death.

The attack by Corlett's XIX Corps on the western side of the Vire River was focused in the 29th Division sector. Although a push along the St Lô–Bayeux road might have seemed the obvious route into the city, the division had found that the road was too vulnerable due to German observation from hills to the south. As a result, Gen. Gebhardt shifted his focus to the center where the 116th Infantry could use the cover offered by the northern slopes of the Martinville Ridge to reduce its vulnerability to artillery fire. By this stage, the 3. Fallschirmjäger-Division was in a perilous state, with only about a third of its combat strength and its FS-Rgt. 9 largely destroyed in the previous fighting. The FS-Rgt. 8 was moved into its place, reinforced by an improvised unit formed from troops of the divisional signals company.

On Saturday, July 15, the 116th Infantry advanced faster than the division's other two regiments, and 2/116th Infantry leapfrogged ahead on the St Lô–Bayeux road by an indirect approach over the Martinville Ridge. As a result, the two lead battalions of 116th Infantry were in an exposed salient that became the target of German counter-attacks on the 16th. The previous fighting had been so costly that Co. A, 1/116th Infantry was commanded by a sergeant. Even when a new commander and some reinforcements arrived on the 18th, the company only numbered 23 men of whom only six were from the original group; its nominal strength should have been 275 men. The 2/116th was in a precarious position on the St Lô road, isolated from the rest of the division and subjected to repeated German attacks.

Medics move Capt. John Strader to a jeep ambulance on July 19 during the fighting north of St Lô. Strader, the executive officer of Co. A, 134th Infantry, 35th Division, had been wounded by shrapnel two days earlier but had returned to combat after the company commander was severely wounded. He led the company for two days before being incapacitated when hit in the leg by sniper fire. He was later awarded the Silver Star for his actions on those two days.

The town of St Lô had been devastated by air bombardment and artillery shelling. This is the view seen by US Army units on entering the city from the north-east. The Dollée stream had become blocked by all the rubble, creating a small, fetid lake.

In spite of the dangerous isolation of two battered battalions of the 116th Infantry, the situation on the German side was grim. The 352. Infanterie-Division had been reduced to a combat strength of about 2,100 men and a significant fraction of these troops was suffering from combat exhaustion due to the unrelenting fighting. The 35th Division had continued its slow push down along the east side of the Vire River against the 352. Infanterie-Division, but the eastward turn of the Vire above St Lô threatened to push the Germans against the river where they might become trapped. All the available

Shortly before leading the final attack against St Lô on July 17, Maj. Thomas Howie, the popular commander of the 3rd Battalion, 116th Infantry, 29th Division telephoned the divisional commander, Gen. Gebhardt, saying he would meet him in the city. He was killed in a mortar barrage that day. Gebhardt insisted that the lead jeep into the city carry his body to the town's Saint Croix Cathedral, making him the first American soldier to enter the city. This image of the flag-draped body was widely published in the United States, but due to wartime censorship, was identified only as the "Major of St. Lô."

Task Force C enters St Lô on the afternoon of July 18, passing by Café-Restaurant Malherbe near the Carrefour de la Bascule crossroads. The M4 tank was from the 747th Tank Battalion and troops of the 1/115th Infantry, 29th Division.

bridges over the Vire had been downed by American air or artillery attack except for one. This surviving bridge, the Pont de Gourfaleur near Baudre, was south of St Lô and so of no use for retreating over the river. Furthermore, it had been damaged. The attacks by the 35th Division, along with the penetrations across the Vire in the VII Corps sector by the 30th Division threatened to completely unhinge the 352.Infanterie-Division's defenses.

This is the same Carrefour de la Bascule crossroads in St Lô later on Tuesday, July 18. Maj. Glover S. Johns had set up the command post of the 1/115th Infantry in the restaurant building to the right. The area came under fire from a German anti-tank gun to the west along Rue de Neufbourg. Capt. Sydney Vincent, the commander of Co. B, 803rd Tank Destroyer Battalion, moved his M10 3in. GMC, seen here on the left, around the corner of the building to try to silence the gun. The vehicle was knocked out by return fire but Vincent and his crew escaped. German mortar fire soon followed and Vincent was killed moments later behind the vehicle. He was posthumously awarded the Silver Star for his actions that day. The second M10 tank destroyer, to the right, was also knocked out during this gun duel.

During the late afternoon of Monday, July 17, Hausser warned the Heeresgruppe B headquarters that the 352. Infanterie-Division would soon have to withdraw into the northern outskirts of St Lô or risk encirclement. At 1755hrs, the operations officer of Heeresgruppe B, Oberst Hans von Tempelhof, responded that Hausser should use his own discretion. There was considerable turmoil in the office since Rommel had been wounded earlier in the day by a strafing Spitfire. Kluge took over Rommel's responsibilities late in the day and was briefed on the situation around 2100hrs, and he subsequently approved the establishment of a new main-line-of-resistance. Kluge informed GFM Alfred Jodl of the Wehrmacht high command in Berlin about these developments after the fact since Berlin was dogmatically opposed to any withdrawals, no matter how prudent and inevitable. The 352. Infanterie-Division began pulling out of its positions on the night of July 17–18. When the 35th Division resumed its attacks on Tuesday morning, it found the previous main-line-of-resistance to have been abandoned.

The collapse of the 352. Infanterie-Division defenses on the north side of St Lô convinced Gen. Gebhardt that the time was right for a hard push for the city. The assistant divisional commander, Gen. Norman Cota, had organized

Task Force C (Cota) for this mission, consisting of the 29th Reconnaissance Troop, supported by a tank platoon of the 747th Tank Battalion, Co. B of the 803rd Tank Destroyer Battalion, along with engineer and other troops. The Task Force totaled about 600 men and was heavily motorized. The morning attacks on the 18th by the 115th Infantry along the boundary with the 35th Division advanced unusually rapidly and, as a result, at 1430hrs, Gebhardt instructed Cota to activate Task Force C to join with 1/115th Infantry and head into the city.

The M8 armored cars of Lt. Edward Jones' 29th Reconnaissance Troop were the first troops into the city and they began to deploy to pre-arranged road junctions starting at 1800hrs. The city had been the target of numerous bomber and artillery strikes, leaving it a ruin with its streets clogged with rubble. Although the Germans did not intend to defend the town in force aside from some rear guards, Task Force C was hit by artillery and mortar fire from the neighboring sectors.

By this point, the 275. Infanterie-Division had finally arrived from Brittany. Hausser refused to deploy the division east of the Vire near St Lô due to the greater threat posed by VII Corps west of the river. He did provide one battalion to reinforce the failing 352. Infanterie-Division on July 18. This was used to stage a counter-attack to retake St Lô late on Tuesday. The preparations for this attack were spotted by outposts of the 115th Infantry and the attack was crushed with artillery fire before it built up any momentum.

The 113th Cavalry Group, in XIX Corps reserve, was sent through St Lô in the early hours of Wednesday 19 July, probing for the new German main-line-of-resistance outside the city. It was soon found that the 352. Infanterie-Division had set up a new defense line on the hills immediately south of St Lô. The rest of the 115th Infantry entered St Lô and began cleaning up German stragglers.

The wreck of an SdKfz 231 heavy armored car of Panzeraufklärungs-Abteilung 130 of the Panzer-Lehr-Division abandoned on the streets of St Lô after the fighting.

THE AFTERMATH

The Battle of the Hedgerows involved no dramatic advances or decisive maneuvers. It was a grinding battle of attrition. A US Army study of the hedgerow fighting concluded that "The real heroes of this fighting were the soldiers, the platoon leaders and the company commanders. They met the enemy, they made the decisions which won and lost the host of little battles which added up to the Battle of the Hedgerows. Superficially resembling position warfare, and at least as bloody, actually this mode of fighting was a war of movement. Seldom has the outcome of battle rested more completely on individual valor and the initative of the small unit commander."

US casualties in the Battle of the Hedgerows were unexpectedly high, about 40,000 men including about 7,200 killed and 30,000 wounded. A US Army survey of several infantry divisions between June 6 and July 31, 1944 found that rifle companies on average suffered casualties of 60 percent of their enlisted men and 68 percent of their officers. Bradley later remarked that "we had estimated that the infantry would incur 70 percent of the losses of combat forces. By August we had boosted that figure to 83 percent on the basis of our experience in the Normandy hedgerows." For example, in 15 days of fighting around St Lô, the 30th Division sustained 3,934 battle casualties, a loss rate of 25 percent for the unit as a whole but 90 percent of its rifle platoon strength.

From the perspective of its original plans, the First US Army's three-week "Battle of the Hedgerows" failed to reach its geographic objectives. Although Bradley had originally anticipated a relatively quick push on the right flank by VIII and VII Corps, the tenacious German defense and the difficulties of operating in the marshes and *bocage* slowed the pace of the assault. Yet the failure to reach specific geographic objectives was largely irrelevant as the requirements had been met for the impending Operation *Cobra* break-out. The First US Army had reached adequate starting points out of the worst areas of swamp and hedgerow.

By far the most essential consequence of the Battle of the Hedgerows was the fatal impact it had on 7. Armee as would become evident after the launch of Operation *Cobra* on Tuesday, July 25. Detailed casualty figures for the 7. Armee in the Battle of the Hedgerows are lacking. Its combat effective strength fell from a peak of about 46,000 to about 26,000 by the third week of July. Total German casualties in France up to the start of Operation *Cobra* on July 25 were 116,863 men including 10 generals and 158 senior commanders. Since OB West casualties in France up to the end of June 1944 were 35,454, this suggests that casualties in the first three weeks of July in both the American and British sectors were 81,409. OB West had received only 27,125 replacements of which only 10,078 had actually reached the front, leading to impossible shortages of troops in many combat units.

The Battle of the Hedgerows crippled nearly all of the infantry divisions in 84. Korps. With the exception of the newly arrived 275. Infanterie-Division, all were rated by Choltitz's 84. Korps headquarters as having a combat value of only 3 (suitable for defense), 4 (limited suitability for defense) or less. Even the elite Panzer formations in the corps were exhausted. Operation *Cobra* was focused against the Panzer-Lehr-Division which was rated at a combat value of "3." Of its available six Panzergrenadier battalions, three were rated as weak, two as exhausted and one was merely a cadre of the field replacement battalion. The division's combat strength was only about 2,210 troops plus another 1,000 from attached units such as Fallschirmjäger-Regiment 14. Tank strength was equally meager with only 12 PzKpfw IV and 16 Panther tanks still operational. The neighboring 17. SS-Panzergrenadier-Division was assessed by 84. Korps as having a combat strength of only "4," with only 1,400 combat effectives. Of its eight Panzergrenadier battalions, two were rated as weak, five as exhausted, and one was a cadre of the field replacement battalion. Heavy losses in its vehicle force left it with barely 30 percent of its mobility and it had only ten of its original 42 StuG IV assault guns operational. The 2. SS-Panzer-Division was the only division in 84. Korps to receive a rating of "1," but it was too far away from the Operation *Cobra* penetration zone to affect the course of the ensuing battle.

The Wehrmacht's failure to reconstitute its forces in lower Normandy had a variety of causes. From the strategic perspective, the Allies' Operation *Fortitude* deception plan continued to have crippling tactical consequences. The specter of a second Allied amphibious operation by Patton's phantom First Army Group continued to haunt German planners. The 7. Armee was unable to move many of its divisions from Brittany to Normandy due to lingering fears that a second Allied amphibious landing might occur there. Likewise, on the eastern flank, anxiety over a possible Allied landing on the Pas-de-Calais kept the 15. Armee largely in place on the North Sea coast. These anxieties did not disappear until August, after the start of Operation *Cobra*, when Patton's Third US Army suddenly appeared in the race for Brittany. By then it was too late.

To make matters worse, the Battle of the Hedgerows forced Hausser into a slap-dash defensive scheme that made 7. Armee ripe for breakthrough. Kluge was unhappy that Hausser was keeping two infantry divisions, the 265. Infanterie-Division and 353. Infanterie-Division, as his reserves instead of the Panzer and Panzergrenadier divisions. In the event of a breakthrough, the infantry divisions would not have the mobility to respond. Hausser had been forced into this deployment since the continual American attacks had prevented withdrawing the Panzer units into the reserves on several occasions. Nevertheless, Hausser failed to rectify the situation during the interlude between the fall of St Lô on July 18 and the start of Operation *Cobra* on July 24–25. In the event, Kluge was so focused on the British threat that he did not pressure Hausser to make essential changes in the American sector. This fatal disposition became evident during the Operation *Cobra* breakthrough.

To further distract Kluge from the St Lô problems, the British Second Army launched yet another offensive, Operation *Goodwood*, on July 18, 1944, the same day as the capture of St Lô. Under such circumstances, Kluge's headquarters as well as the high command in Berlin remained focused on the Caen sector and not on the St Lô one. The German high command's focus was further diverted on Thursday, July 20, when a group of German Army officers centered in the Replacement Army (Ersatzheer) attempted to assassinate Hitler at his East Prussia headquarters. Although Kluge was not directly involved in the bomb plot he was aware of the scheme. A witch hunt soon began in Berlin to round up anyone with suspected involvement and both Kluge and Rommel would eventually become caught up.

Kluge tried to convince Hitler of the gravity of the situation in Normandy, but to no avail. On July 23, Hitler received a message from Kluge that concluded "the moment is approaching when despite all efforts, the hard-pressed front will break. In view of the inadequate mobility of our forces, when the enemy has erupted into open terrain, orderly and effective conduct of the battle will become impossible."

Hitler was still suffering the effects of the July 20 bomb blast, but he would have been unlikely to accept Kluge's advice any way. Hitler's tactical response to the Allied advances was inevitably another counter-offensive. As often as not, these served to further undermine the German defenses. Hitler continually gravitated towards a large offensive by Panzergruppe West against the British as the only action likely to push the Allies back into the sea. A basic plan had been outlined by Rommel on July 15 involving seven Panzer divisions, and Hitler issued instructions for a surprise Panzergruppe West night attack to take place on August 1. Although this attack never took place, it undermined the chances for reinforcements of the beleaguered St Lô front.

In order to conduct the August 1 attack, it was necessary to substitute infantry divisions for Panzer divisions in the Panzergruppe West sector, draining the Heeresgruppe B reserve and tying down the few available infantry divisions that might have been used to reinforce the St Lô sector. It also required the diversion of 149 PzKpfw IV Ausf. Hs, 76 Panthers, 19 Tigers, and 15 StuG IIIs to bring these units up to strength prior to the attack, essentially sucking away all the replacements for other sectors of the Normandy front.

Reserving the Panzer Divisions

Division	Relief date	Substitute Division
9. SS-Panzer-Division	July 10	277. Infanterie-Division
1. SS-Panzer-Division	Night, July 13–14	272. Infanterie-Division
12. SS-Panzer-Division	Night, July 13–14	272. Infanterie-Division
10. SS-Panzer-Division	July 17	271. Infanterie-Division
Panzer-Lehr-Division	July 18	5. Fallschirmjäger-Division
2. Panzer-Division	July 22	326. Infanterie-Division

In the event, Operation *Cobra* pre-empted the August 1 Panzer offensive. Instead, these Panzer forces were used to conduct Operation *Lüttich* later in August. This was Hitler's scheme to crush Operation *Cobra* by a Panzer offensive to the sea at Avranches, thereby cutting off the American spearheads. This attack was crushed in the battle of Mortain between August 7 and 13 by the 30th Division. The Caen sector was so weakened by the diversion of the Panzer force that the British 21st Army Group was finally able to break through and begin its drive on Falaise. It was another critical step in the destruction of the Wehrmacht in Normandy.

THE BATTLEFIELD TODAY

Normandy is a popular destination for military history buffs, though the vast majority of visitors go to see the D-Day invasion beaches. There are few popular destinations related to the Battle of the Hedgerows. The hedgerow terrain still exists, but the extent of the hedgerows has been greatly reduced since the war due to agricultural modernization in the region over the past seven decades.

St Lô serves as the symbolic site for the commemoration of the battles even though most of the fighting took place outside the town. The city itself was badly damaged during the war and has been heavily reconstructed. There are numerous memorial plaques scattered around the town, but the

This massive bunker on Place du Champ de Mars in St Lô was a major telephone exchange for the Wehrmacht in lower Normandy. During the final days of the fighting for St Lô it was occupied by Hptm. Loges of Grenadier-Regiment 916, 352. Infanterie-Division. It still exists today, but submerged under the Salle de Sports Fernand Beaufils and other buildings on the north side of the plaza.

TOMBE A LA TÊTE DE SES TROUPES EN LIBERANT NOTRE VILLE
AU CRI DE RALLIEMENT... A SAINT/LO!

There are numerous monuments to the 1944 fighting in Lower Normandy. One of the best known is this memorial to the "Major of St. Lô," Thomas Howie, located at the intersection of Rue Maréchal Juin and Rue Maréchal de Lattre de Tassigny in St Lô, on the former Carrefour de la Bascule shown in photographs earlier in this book. (Kevin Hymel)

"Major of St. Lô" monument to Maj. Howie is no doubt the most visited. The ever-useful *After the Battle* magazine devoted one of its issues, Number 138 (2007), to the battle for St Lô, and this provides a useful guide for anyone wishing to visit the town.

For hardcore military history buffs wishing to see the sites of the more important battles and skirmishes covered in this book, Peter Yates' book in the *Battlezone Normandy* series is a very useful guide.

Bocage is still common throughout lower Normandy today, but many of the hedgerows have been reduced or removed to facilitate modern farming techniques. This is a typical example of a rural road with hedgerows on either side.

FURTHER READING

The Battle of the Hedgerows is covered in two official US Army histories. The Blumenson volume *Breakout and Pursuit* in the Army "Green Book" series provides a comprehensive overview of the campaign. The earlier 1946 study *St.-Lo* focuses on the XIX Corps operations and so offers more detail on some aspects of the fighting. US Army after-action reports and other official unit records are in Records Group 407 at the National Archives and Records Administration1 (NARA) in College Park, Maryland. Also noteworthy is a separate collection in Records Group 407 called "Combat Interviews" that contain first-hand reports collected by army historians from combat troops immediately after the battles. The Fort Benning Maneuver Center has a collection of the reports prepared immediately after the war at the Infantry School and the Fort Knox Armor School by officers who served in the campaign and they are available on-line. For readers interested in a first-hand account of hedgerow fighting, there is none better than Glover Johns' *The Clay Pigeons of St. Lo*. Johns took command of the 1/115th Infantry in the middle of July and led the battalion into St. Lô with Task Force C.

There is no overview of the hedgerow fighting from the German perspective though there are a wealth of sources. A number of internal studies by James Hodgson of the US Army Center of Military History were prepared for the Foreign Military Studies program in their little-known "R" series." These are essentially chapter-by-chapter background briefings to illuminate the German side of the operations in support of Blumenson's official US Army history. Based on captured German records, they provide a great deal of detail on German organization and decision making. They are available in Record Group 319 at NARA. Also at NARA, Record Group 242 contains captured German records, on microfilm, with a great deal of material on the campaign such as the 7. Armee Kriegstagebuch (war diary); corps and divisional records in the collection are quite sparse. There are also a few Foreign Military Studies reports on units involved in the campaign, most notably the series on the 352. Infanterie-Division.

US Army Foreign Military Studies
Gersdorff, Rudolf Freiherr von, *The Campaign in Northern France 25 Jul 1944–14 Sep 1944*, FMS B-722 (1946)
Hodgson, James, *The Battle of France: 21 July–25 August 1944 (Chapter VI)*, FMS R-58 (1955)
Hodgson, James, *The Battle of the Hedgerows (Chapter IV)*, FMS R-54 (1954)
Hodgson, James, *The Eve of Defeat: 18 July–End of July (Chapter V)*, FMS R-57 (1954)
Hodgson, James, *The German Defense of Normandy: The Situation at the Beginning of July 1944 (Chapter II)*, FMS R-24 (1953)
Hodgson, James, *The Germans in Normandy, 1 July 1944: Before the Offensive (Chapter III)*, FMS R-49 (1954)
Hodgson, James, *Sequence of Essential Events in the Fall of St. Lo*, FMS R-84 (1955)
Mahlmann, Paul, *353.Infanterie-Division*, FMS A-983 (1946)
Schimpf, Richard, *Operations of the 3 FS Division during the Invasion in France June–August 1944*, FMS B-541 (1947)
Ziegelmann, Fritz, *The 352.Infanterie-Division: The Fighting from 23 June to 10 July 1944*, FMS B-439 (1947)
Ziegelmann, Fritz, *The 352.Infanterie-Division: The Battles from 11 to 18 July 1944*, FMS B-455 (1947)
Ziegelmann, Fritz, *The 352.Infanterie-Division: The Battle South of St. Lo*, FMS B-464 (1947)

US Army Reports

Browning, Maj. Earl, *Operations of the 29th Infantry Division in the Attack and Capture of St. Lo, France, 13–18 July 1944* (Ft Benning Infantry School, 1950)

Bruce, Maj. Oliver, *The Operations of the 3rd Battalion, 134th Infantry (35th Infantry Division) in the Attack on St. Lo, France, 15–18 July 1944,* (Ft Benning Infantry School, 1950)

Campbell, Maj. William, *Tanks with Infantry: Methods learned and employed by the 1st Infantry Division and the 745th Tank Battalion* (Ft Knox Armor School, 1947)

Folsom, Capt. Charles, *Hedgerow Fighting near Carentan: 329th Infantry, 30th Division* (Ft Knox Armor School, 1948)

Lee, Maj. Ray, *The Operations of the 23rd Infantry (2nd Infantry Division) in the Attack on Hill 192, East of St. Lo, 11–12 July 1944,* (Ft Benning Infantry School, 1948)

Richmond, Maj. Budd, *The Operation of the 3rd Battalion, 137th Infantry (35th Infantry Division) in the Vicinity of St. Lo, France 11–15 July 1944* (Ft Benning Infantry School, 1950)

Ziegler, Capt. Clarence, *The Operations of 2nd Battalion, 329th Infantry (83rd Infantry Division) in the Attack along the Road to Periers, 4 July 1944* (Ft Benning Infantry School, 1950)

Books

Balkoski, Joseph, *Beyond the Beachhead: The 29th Infantry Division in Normandy* (Stackpole: 1989)

Bernage, Georges, *Objectif La Haye-du-Puits, 3–9 juillet 1944* (Heimdal: 2012)

Bernage, Georges, *Objectif Saint-Lô, 7–18 juillet 1944* (Heimdal: 2011)

Blumenson, Martin, *Breakout and Pursuit* (Center of Military History: 1961)

Colby, John, *War from the Ground Up: The 90th Division in WWII* (Nortex: 1991)

Doubler, Michael, *Busting the Bocage: American Combined Arms Operations in France 6 June–31 July 1944* (Combat Studies Institute: 1988)

Doubler, Michael, *Closing with the Enemy: How GIs Fought the War in Europe 1944–45* (University Press of Kansas: 1994)

Hinsley, F. H., et al., *British Intelligence in the Second World War, Vol. 3, Part 2* (HMSO: 1988)

Hogan, David, *A Command Post at War: First Army Headquarters in Europe 1943–1945* (Center of Military History: 2000)

Isby, David, *Fighting the Invasion: The German Army from D-Day to Villers Bocage* (Greenhill, 2001)

Johns, Glover, *The Clay Pigeons of St. Lo* (Stackpole: 1958)

Lodieu, Dider, *Dying for St.-Lô: Hedgerow Hell, July 1944* (Histoire & Collections: 2007)

Reardon, Mark (ed.), *Defending Fortress Europe: The War Diary of the German 7th Army in Normandy: 6 June to 26 July 1944* (Aberjona: 2012)

Sylvan, William, Smith, Francis, *Normandy to Victory: The War Diary of Courtney Hodges & the First US Army* (University Press of Kentucky: 2008)

Weidinger, Otto, *2.SS-Panzer-Division Das Reich, Vol. V* (Fedorowicz: 2012)

Wind, M., Günther, H. (ed.), *Kriegstagebuch 17.SS-Panzergrenadier-Division "Götz von Berlichingen"* (Schild Verlag: 1993)

Wood, James (ed.), *Army of the West: The Weekly Reports of German Army Group B from Normandy to the West Wall* (Stackpole: 2007)

Yates, Peter, *Battlezone Normandy: Battle for St.-Lo* (Sutton: 2004)

The Cross of Lorraine: A Combat History of the 79th Infantry Division, June 1942–December 1945 (US Army: 1946)

First United States Army: Report of Operations, 20 October 1943–1 August 1944. (Vols 1–7), (US Army: 1944)

Die Geschichte der 352.Infanterie-Division (Kameradschaft: n.d.)

St.-Lo (7 July–19 July 1944), (War Department: 1946)

INDEX

Note: page locators in bold refer to illustrations, captions and plates.